ETHIOPIA

'And then the dispossessed were drawn west . . . families, tribes, dusted out, tractored out. Car-loads, caravans, homeless and hungry; twenty thousand and fifty thousand and a hundred thousand and two hundred thousand. They streamed over the mountains, hungry and restless—restless as ants scurrying to find work to do—to lift, to push, to pull, to pick, to cut—anything, any burden to bear, for food. . . .'

John Steinbeck, *The Grapes of Wrath*, 1939.

'Many millions of people in the poor countries are going to starve to death before our eyes. We will see them doing so on our television sets.'

C. P. Snow, 1969.

ETHIOPIA

The Challenge of Hunger

by

GRAHAM HANCOCK

Part of the proceeds from this publication is being donated to Oxfam and Christian Aid for the relief of suffering in Ethiopia

LONDON
VICTOR GOLLANCZ LTD
1985

First published in Great Britain 1985
by Victor Gollancz Ltd,
14 Henrietta Street, London WC2E 8QJ

Copyright © Graham Hancock 1985

British Library Cataloguing in Publication Data
Hancock, Graham
  Ethiopia: the challenge of hunger.
  1. Ethiopia—Famines
  I. Title
  363.3'492   HC845.Z9F3

ISBN 0-575-03680-X
ISBN 0-575-03681-8 Pbk

Photoset by Rowland Phototypesetting Ltd,
Bury St Edmunds, Suffolk
Printed in Great Britain by
Billing and Son Ltd, Worcester

Contents

Acknowledgements

The faults of this book and the views expressed in it are my own. If it has merits then these have a lot to do with the excellent research for the project done at great speed by my friend and colleague Enver Carim. I would also like to acknowledge my appreciation of the help of Dr Richard Pankhurst who gave me access to his unique studies on the history of famine in Ethiopia on which I drew heavily in writing the chapter entitled 'The Curse of Famine'. While I was in Ethiopia visiting the drought-affected areas, I learned much that was of value from my travelling companions Tom Kelly and Dr Joseph Kennedy of the American voluntary agency Africaire. I would also like to put on record my appreciation of the invaluable help and information provided by the Relief and Rehabilitation Commission in Addis Ababa, an organization that has done an unparalleled job in saving human life during the current emergency. Finally, warmest thanks and appreciation to Carol, and to my mother and father, who read and commented on the manuscript page by page over Christmas and the New Year while I was writing.

Okehampton
January 1985

Introduction

A culture is dying in Ethiopia. A complete way of life, virtually unassailed for 3000 years, is coming to an end. The Abyssinian high plateau, known to the ancient Greeks as a 'cool celestial island', is turning to dust, merging wearily into the barren and stony deserts that surround it. As it does so, the human populations that it has supported for so long are blowing away too. Having slaughtered their draught oxen and eaten their seed grain, the people are leaving forever their eroded fields and terraces and pouring in countless thousands into squalid, under-supplied feeding camps.

Such things have happened before—in other countries, to other people. But possibly they have never happened on such a scale and certainly they have never happened amidst such a glare of publicity. In the global village to which television has reduced our world, the tragedy of the Ethiopian drought has been played out each night in our own living rooms. Sandwiched between advertisements for personal computers, new cars, Coca Cola and next summer's holiday, we have witnessed the lines of the hungry, the mothers hopelessly dangling shrunken nipples into the listless mouths of their dying babies, children wasted with marasmus, once proud adults now destitute and ashamed.

Reports of what was happening in Ethiopia made television news several times during the first nine months of 1984, but public reaction was small and editors gave the story little play. On 23 October, however, a seven-minute film by Visnews cameraman Mohamed Amin, with commentary by reporter Michael Buerk, was shown throughout the day on BBC news bulletins, and was subsequently picked up and networked around the world. This film, shot on location in the towns of Makalle and Korem in northern Ethiopia, portrayed a horrific human disaster on a scale that readily summoned up images of

Hiroshima and Nagasaki, a disaster of hunger and suffering so great that it seemed to call into question the entire international system of aid, co-operation and control by which mankind governs its affairs in the late twentieth century. The patient, starved faces of those who were about to die, the weak cries of the infants, the terrible spectacle of the feeding centres without food and the clinics without medicines, all these things together seemed to proclaim: 'Here God, if ever there was one, is a case for a miracle.'

To this supplication, and in the apparent absence of God, the international community has now responded by constructing a tremendous juggernaut of emergency aid and setting it rolling in the direction of Ethiopia. Big business, too, has got in on the act, not least in the form of press baron Robert Maxwell who, like a fifth horseman of the apocalypse, turned up in Addis Ababa in November 1984 in the saddle of the *Daily Mirror* million-dollar mercy flight. On a smaller scale, individuals all over the world have dug deep into their pockets and produced an avalanche of charitable coin, blankets, second-hand clothes and high-energy biscuits.

What was so special about Mohamed Amin's film that it was able to get this remarkable show on the road when all other efforts during 1984—not only by the press, but also by voluntary agencies like Oxfam, and by the Ethiopians themselves—had signally failed to excite the least bit of attention? On this point, Amin is quite clear: 'There was absolutely nothing special about the film. It was the suffering that the film depicted that was special.' A hardbitten newsman who has been reporting Africa and its disasters for more than twenty years, he told me: 'I've never filmed anything on this scale and I've never filmed anything that has moved me in the way that this did. I've filmed wars, executions, deaths—none of it has ever touched me. But this time it was different. I cried when I was editing this film, I actually broke down and cried.'

Amin and I are close friends, and we have worked on several projects together in many parts of Ethiopia over the years. As we talked in Addis Ababa, prior to my own first visit to the drought-affected areas, I began to get some premonition of the epic nature of the phenomenon that I would be witnessing:

In one place that we filmed in Makalle [Amin told me] there was a patch of ground, like a sheep-pen, surrounded by a low stone wall about four feet high. Grouped inside this wall there were maybe 150 starving people who, for no special reason, had been selected to be fed and to receive blankets. Outside the wall there were about 10,000 other people, just as starved, just as near to death, who were not going to get fed that day, or the next day, and maybe were not going to get fed at all because there was almost no food in Makalle at that time. Anyway, the officials went round inside the wall handing out grain, tins of donated butter, blankets and second-hand clothes to the lucky hundred and fifty. The others outside, who were virtually being condemned to death, just stood there, the front ones leaning on the wall, they just stood there and watched what was happening without any kind of greed or resentment. I think it was this calmness, this passivity, that got to me because I knew that if I had been in their position, with maybe my own child dying, I would not have just stood there and watched others be given the chance of life. I think I would have done anything, rioted, killed, to get the food I needed.

If Makalle was bad, Korem was much worse:

There were about 60,000 starving people in Korem when we arrived, camped in an open field outside the town. There was almost no food, and no real shelter, and the nights up there are cold, with temperatures falling to around zero. The early morning scenes were the worst, by far the worst thing I have ever seen. There was this tremendous mass of people, groaning and weeping, scattered across the ground in the dawn mist. I don't really know how to describe it but the thing that came to my mind at the time was that it was as if a hundred jumbo jets had crashed and spilled out the bodies of their passengers amongst the wreckage, the dead and the living mixed together so you couldn't tell one from the other. It still shatters me when I think back on what I saw. During the night, while I had slept, people had been slowly and steadily dying of exposure, and there they were in this field—a mother cradling a dead child, a brother holding tight to the body of his dead sister, a husband and a wife, dressed in rags, dead together on the ground. I went and filmed in the mortuary where the dead were carried by their relatives to be logged and recorded, and for two solid hours the bodies kept on being brought in. To the people at Korem, just to survive the night was an achievement.

Whilst in Addis, waiting for a travel permit to visit Korem and the other drought-affected areas myself, I asked a number of friends and colleagues who had already had direct contact with the famine victims to give me their own impressions. Like Amin, they all spoke in epic terms, their voices falling to an awed whisper as they talked. Each clearly felt that he had been witness to, and had somehow participated in, something momentous and quite unprecedented. Again and again I was reminded of Hiroshima and Nagasaki. Was this how the survivors of the nuclear holocaust talked as they recalled the devastation they had seen around them?

One Ethiopian friend told me:

On the road from Kombolcha, nearly all the way to Addis Ababa, a journey of 400 kilometres, I saw nothing growing at all. The land had been plucked bare. The fields were empty. Everywhere people were on the move, those who still had the strength to do so desperately searching for food. In that whole area, there was nothing, just nothing to eat. Even the wild animals and the birds were starving.

What impressed him most, he said, was the courage of the people, the small attempts at generosity and dignity in the midst of the wasteland:

I remember there was one mother and her small boy, both really starved, really sick, just sitting under a tree waiting to die. I gave the child some bread I was carrying, but instead of eating it himself he offered it to his mother. She was too far gone even to take it. The child pushed it to her lips, but she refused it. Then he looked at the bread again himself, just looked at it for a long while, and finally he dropped it down onto the road. It was as though he were saying 'What's the point? Even if you feed me today, I will still be dead tomorrow'.

In the town of Efeson, my friend said, he met a housewife who had taken in an orphaned baby. She had been standing in her doorway one day when a thin peasant carrying a ragged bundle had walked by.

'What are you carrying?' she had asked the peasant.

'This?' he replied, indicating the bundle. 'It's just a baby. Its mother and father died and I'm carrying it until it dies also. It's a human being like you and me, so I can't throw it away.'

'Would you let me have the child?' the housewife asked.

'Yes,' said the peasant, 'God's blessings on you.' And without further ado he handed his bundle over and went on his way.

'When I was in Efeson,' my friend concluded, 'the child had already been there for about three weeks. He was very young, not even of weaning age, but somehow his adopted family were managing to feed him. Please look for him if you go there and tell me what has become of him. I often wonder if he lived or if he died.'

In individual tragedies, each one multiplied a thousandfold, it is possible to discern the human outlines of the greater tragedy afflicting Ethiopia today. In this country of 42 million people more than *seven million* are already directly affected by drought, have already been touched, to a greater or lesser degree, by the pangs of hunger. And big though these figures are, what is perhaps even more stunning is the realization that Ethiopia is not alone, that many other countries in Africa are just as seriously affected. The entire region known as the Sahel, that necklace of desperately poor nations suspended across the continent just below the Sahara desert, has for centuries been undergoing a process of vicious environmental degradation. In the last 20 years, this process has produced conditions of almost permanent drought: topsoils so denuded that seeds will not germinate, wells drying up, and, everywhere, land that was once good turning to desert. As a result, whole populations of self-sufficient people have been deprived of any possibility of continuing to support themselves and have been rendered abject and dependent. In hell-hole camps, awaiting the daily handouts that barely suffice to keep them alive, every shred of their individuality and uniqueness has been stripped from them. As well as their prosperity, they have lost their history, their folklore, their religion and their culture. Even their humanity itself has been called into question.

The countries of the Sahel were virtually destroyed by drought in the early 1970s, and efforts launched since then to fight the steady encroachment of the Sahara desert have met with little success. Mauritania, Mali, Bourkina Fasso, Niger, Chad and the Sudan form the central core of the region. All of these countries, with the possible exception of Niger, entered 1985 with prospects that were even bleaker than in the worst years of the 1970s. Chad was hit by a devastating drought in 1984, with rainfall down to about one quarter of normal. In Mali, thousands of rural people were reported to be converging on urban centres in search of food. Sudan, by November 1984, was already beginning to suffer a famine almost as severe as Ethiopia's. It was estimated that the Sudanese would require over one million tonnes of relief food in 1985 if mass starvation was to be avoided.

Senegal in West Africa and Ethiopia, Somalia and Djibouti in East Africa, though not traditionally defined as Sahelian countries, are all now suffering typically Sahelian problems of drought and desertification. Even more alarming, it is clear that these problems are beginning to spread. Kenya, Uganda and Tanzania are, today, all potential famine centres. Further south, Botswana has been in the grip of severe drought for five years and Zimbabwe, one of Africa's agricultural powerhouses, has experienced widespread crop failures. In Mozambique, formerly a prosperous Portuguese colony, 100,000 people died of starvation and the effects of malnutrition during 1984. Overall, according to United Nations estimates, some 300 million people out of Africa's total population of 475 million now live under the threat of hunger. In the worst-hit areas, it seems quite certain that at least one million Africans are going to die during 1985 for want of food.

The Ethiopian famine is a part of this broader problem and does not stand in isolation. Nevertheless, it was the calm, the dignity and the fortitude of the starving Ethiopians in the face of avoidable death that appealed most directly to the imagination, conscience and sympathy of the West and that set in motion one of the great emergency aid efforts of modern times. It was one of those very rare occasions in which a majority rather than a minority of Europeans, Americans, Australians and other citizens of the industrialized countries took more than a passing interest in a development issue and, as such, it was certainly a heartening indication that there are still threads of fundamental unity and concern in our divided antagonistic world.

This uplifting view of human nature was amply supported by what I saw when I arrived at Addis Ababa's Bole Airport in November 1984: scores of heavy-duty transporter aircraft with Russian, American, East German, British and a medley of other markings were lined up on the apron loading emergency food supplies to fly in to the drought-affected areas. It was like a vision of all the lofty principles that the United Nations stands for suddenly brought to life, and I could almost hear the swords being beaten into ploughshares.

After a few days in the Ethiopian capital, however, I began to realize that all was not what it seemed. To be sure, the Americans and the British were there, doing a worthwhile job and saving many lives; but, at the same time, their respective governments were basking in the glow of the PR that their good works had won for them and taking every opportunity to point out how much more worthy their own efforts were than those, for example, of the Russians. The Russians for their part, whose first reaction to news of the famine had been to accuse the Western media of a plot to blacken the name of Ethiopia, were now hastily applying a shine to their image by vying to outdo the West in every aspect of disaster relief. On the sidelines, Soviet and Polish camera-crews struggled ruthlessly with ITN and NBC in an endless battle for the best angles from which to film the efforts of their own teams. Amidst all this inter-denominational bitching and back-biting it often seemed that the real reason that everyone was there had been forgotten and that the Ethiopian famine had become nothing more than a hot new front in the Cold War.

Another worrying aspect was the extent to which the famine had been transformed into a 'media event' with its own stage props, its own cast of thousands, and its own rapidly evolving plot. According to this plot, it soon became clear, the heroes of the Ethiopian epic-tragedy were Western governments and relief workers making all kinds of noble sacrifices, taking all kinds of risks, to rescue the hapless drought victims. The villain of the piece at first seemed to be the weather; however, it did not take the media long to identify a new and somewhat more accessible target for the boos and hisses of the audience—the Ethiopian government itself.

One consequence of pinning the blame on Ethiopia's already much maligned Marxist administration was that it absolved Western audiences from any real need to go on feeling guilty about or responsible for what was happening and, at the same time, provided media personalities with a first class pulpit from which to expound the majority view that Africans in general are like errant children who do not yet know how to manage their own affairs and therefore require supervision. Although surely not a supporter of this view himself, George Galloway, Director of War on Want, provided ammunition to those who do support it when, in the *Sunday Times* of 2 December 1984, he wrote of 'the culpability of the Ethiopian government both in the scale of the hunger and in its politically-motivated obstruction of the relief effort.' Accusing the 'ruthless military government in Ethiopia' of 'presiding over a famine of historic proportions, deliberately starving out whole areas of its country,' Galloway insisted: 'The time has come to ensure that any aid given reaches all parts of the country and that a commission is put in to see that the relief effort is handled fairly.'

These were heady accusations, and the proposed solution— namely that the Ethiopian government should surrender its sovereignty in matters of food distribution to some sort of international commission—was equally potent. As I began to research this book, what worried me about the charges that were being levelled by Galloway and others was not so much the question of whether they were valid or not, although this was an issue that I intended to examine very closely, as the possible consequences that they might have. Would such accusations not give the authorities in the West precisely the excuse they were looking for to continue to deny long-term aid to Ethiopia, a country that has been shunned for 10 years because of its pro-Soviet policies? And, in the absence of massive long-term aid (as opposed to massive emergency aid), what hope would there be of implementing the sweeping long-term solutions called for if the challenge of hunger in Ethiopia is ever to be met? It was all very well for the media to cast the Ethiopian regime in the role of folk devil; the 'story' would no doubt be greatly improved by this device. At the same time, however, it was a device that would condemn to death many thousands of Ethiopians who, given constructive long-term assistance, might have had a chance for life after the emergency aid had dried up.

One must always be careful not to give too much credence to the role of the media. Nevertheless, anyone who doubts the power of television and the press to influence events and political behaviour will find a powerful refutation in Ethiopia. A decade ago, in 1974, it was media coverage of another Ethiopian drought that led to the overthrow of Emperor Haile Selassie, the 225th monarch in the Solomonic line, and that put the current regime in power. Jonathan Dimbleby's now famous documentary, *The Hidden Hunger,* exposed the deliberate efforts of the imperial government to keep secret a famine that had raged in the high-lands for two years, killing 200,000 people. Apparently the Emperor had felt that it was in bad taste for the world to know that Ethiopians were dying of hunger. Dimbleby disagreed and made his film, which subsequently was shown on television around the globe. The cumbersome international aid-giving machine trundled into action and Selassie came under increasing pressure to do something for his starving subjects. The already considerable dissent movement within Ethiopia, led by students and Marxist army officers, rallied around this point of view and, bit by bit, chinks began to appear in what had previously been thought of as the indestructible imperial armour. On 11 September 1974 the Dimbleby film, previously banned by the regime, was shown on Ethiopian television provoking a shock-wave of revulsion. At dawn the next day the Emperor, who owned 24 Rolls-Royces, was arrested at his palace by junior officers, bundled into an ignominious Volkswagen, and driven off to detention in an equally ignominious army barracks. He was never seen again.

Plus ça change. The current famine, with its attendant media turbulence, contains within it the potential to overthrow the current government of Ethiopia, the Marxist regime of Colonel Mengistu Haile Mariam. There are many who would regard such an overthrow as an event devoutly to be wished. There are many others, including myself, who, though fully aware of the faults of the regime, believe that the consequences of its demise could be disastrous, not only for Ethiopia but also for the region as a whole.

Whatever the rights and wrongs of this debate, it is clear that the challenge of hunger is the central issue in Ethiopia today, a challenge on which governments stand or fall and within which the lives and happiness of millions of people are caught up. On a wider stage, in the context of the dire poverty and dependence of the Sahel and much of the rest of Africa, this same challenge is a world issue of unparalleled importance. What happens in Ethiopia, therefore, how the world responds to the Ethiopian tragedy, and the lessons to be learned from it, are matters of broad and lasting concern.

PART ONE

Ethiopia in Context

Land over 2000 metres
International Boundary
Administrative Boundary
■ Administrative Capital

Ethiopia

Red Sea

SUDAN

Asmara ■ Massawa
ERITREA
Axum ● Adwa
SIMIEN MTS. ■ TIGRE
GONDER   Makalle
● Gonder   Assab ●
Lake Tana   DJIBOUTI
Lalibela WOLLO REP.
● Dessie Mile ●
GOJJAM Bati ●
BLUE NILE Kombolcha
● Assosa   *R. AWASH*
Efeson ●
WOLLEGA SHOA   Dire Dawa ●
ADDIS Harar ■ Jijiga ●
Gambela ● ABABA
Metu ■ SOMALIA
● Gore ARSSI
ILLUBABOR HARERGHE
RIFT
KAFFA *VALLEY*
LAKES BALE MTS.
Arba Minch ● BALE
GAMO
GOFFA SIDAMO

Gulf of Aden

SOMALIA

0 Kilometres 400

KENYA

CHAPTER ONE

Diversity and Contrasts

Over the last five years I have visited virtually all parts of
Ethiopia, using just about every means of transport: mules and
Shanks's pony, donkey carts, cars and Land-Rovers, single-
engined Cessnas, ancient DC3s and ultra-modern jet aircraft.

Looking back, I know that my best year for Ethiopian travels
was 1983 when I spent 12 weeks in the spring covering about a
thousand kilometres a week, north to south and east to west.
The countryside was in full bloom, the people were bright,
inquisitive and kind, the children were beautiful, brimming with
fun and mischief. But that was before the long rains that did not
come, before the drought really took hold, and everything was
different then. . . .

Ethiopia, more than a million square kilometres in size, is a
topographer's delight. The dominant feature of the country is
the central highland massif which, with its precipitous gorges,
soaring peaks, and eroded buttes and mesas, has provided the
scenery that many have now come to regard as typically 'Abyssinian'. One visitor, Rosita Forbes, summed up the majesty and
magic of the highlands in this piece of purple prose:

> When the old gods reigned in Ethiopia they must have played
> chess with those stupendous crags, for we saw bishops' mitres
> cut in lapis lazuli, castles with the ruby of approaching sunset
> on their turrets, an emerald knight where the forest crept up
> onto the rock, and, far away, a king crowned with sapphires
> and guarded by a row of pawns.

Forbes, who travelled by mule from the old port of Massawa,
on the Red Sea coast, to Lake Tana, the source of the Blue Nile,
was writing about the Simien mountains. By far the most
dramatic segment of the Ethiopian massif, the Simien range

contains Africa's fourth highest peak, Mount Ras Deshen, which rises to 4,543 metres. Additionally, there are huge expanses of Afro-Alpine moorland over 3,000 metres above sea level where unique species of flora and fauna have evolved, adapted to the rigours of the high-altitude ecology.

When I was in the Simiens in 1983 I was astonished to find, not much below the 3,000-metre mark, numerous signs of human habitation: small, tidy villages, grassy meadows providing grazing for sheep, goats and cattle, and terraced hillsides planted with cereals. The traditional inhabitants of this region are the Amharas, speaking the Semitic Amharic tongue which has been adopted as Ethiopia's official language. Of them I wrote in my diary at that time: 'Farmers in a sometimes arid, often cold and none-too-fertile environment that suffers bitterly from erosion, they have a proud code of honour, of hospitality and of self-help which makes them a match for this high and remote homeland.'

They are no longer a match, I regret to say. The Simiens straddle the Ethiopian provinces of Gonder and Tigre, two of the worst affected in the current drought. My proud farmers have been transformed into environmental refugees. The lucky ones, those who survived, now queue with their children in the wretched food lines at government camps.

Geologically, the Simiens are young, the product of volcanic activity during the Oligocene era some 40 million years ago. They are in fact the core of a tremendous outpouring of lava that covered an area of more than 15,000 square kilometres to a depth of several thousand metres.

Twenty million years later, a mere blink of an eye in geological time, similarly potent seismic forces led to the creation of another major feature of the Ethiopian landscape—the great Rift Valley which was the result of a collapse of the earth's crust between two roughly parallel fault lines (and which extends, through Ethiopia, as far as Syria to the north and Mozambique to the south). It was at this time that the Arabian Peninsula, geologically a part of Africa, was sundered from the rest of the continent. Scientists speculate that this process of separation is still going on, gradually moving Arabia eastwards towards the Asian landmass and severing much of the Horn of Africa which one day, millions of years in the future, may form the basis of a new continent.

My first journey into the Rift Valley opened my eyes to an

important fact about Ethiopia that I had previously not fully grasped. The human diversity of this country—and it is surely one of the most diverse in Africa—is very much a product of diverse topography. In the space of less than an hour's travel by car, following winding roads eastwards from the town of Dessie, which stands at an altitude of 2,500 metres on the edge of the central escarpment, towards the Rift Valley settlement of Mile, the clear invigorating air of the mountains was left behind to be replaced by the desiccating heat of savannah and then by desert. Through the diminishing hillscapes that pointed the way to the valley floor, I saw that the familiar patterns of settled agriculture, the small, regular family plots that are the hallmark of the highlands, had abruptly vanished. They had been replaced, I noted in my diary, by 'the harsher realities of pastoral nomadism in a land where camels browse and fierce tribesmen jealously guard their cattle and water rights.'

The fierce tribesmen I referred to were the Afar, a nomadic people also known as the Danakil, whom I was to come to love and respect. Their homeland, in the northern sector of the Ethiopian Rift, is without a doubt one of the world's most hostile environments. By contrast to the cold and lofty places of the escarpment, there are points here more than 100 metres below sea level where noon-time temperatures can exceed 50 degrees centigrade. Here, too, amidst yellow and reeking sulphur fields, there are several still-active volcanoes, dying reminders of the past furies that once ravaged this zone and bequeathed to it a burnt and blackened landscape that seems carved from hell.

It appeared to me miraculous that anyone could survive in such conditions. Yet the Afars did more than survive—they prospered. Their principal camel market at Bati, roughly half-way between Dessie and Mile, was a joyous place where hides and skins, salt bars, cattle, camels and goats, were offered for sale by dark-eyed, half-naked women with the proudly beautiful, stately bearing that nomadic life seems to engender.

I have to confess that the image of the Afar warrior following his herds through the badlands of the Rift, a walking stick in one hand and, as often as not, a Kalashnikov in the other, came, as my acquaintance with these people grew, to take on something of the idealized glow of Rousseau's noble savage. I wrote in my diary:

Naturally shy of all strangers, but ready to offer friendship and warmth once their suspicions are allayed, the Afar have, in their simple, austere lifestyle, much to teach industrialized man. Sparing, careful use of the resources at their disposal, ingenuity in overcoming the challenges of nature, courage in the face of adversity, an indomitable will that refuses to accept defeat or humiliation, a soaring, restless spirit that ever seeks for greener pastures—these are the central values of their culture, values which, in their wider context, have made the human race masters of the earth, sea and skies, values which, for all our modern complacency, we forget at our peril.

There are no more noble savages in the Rift today. The 1984 drought, which swept the highland provinces like the Angel of Death on Passover, has also swept the lowlands carrying all before it. Their cattle and goats gone, their plump camel herds reduced to a few sickly beasts, the Afar have become beggars. Fate has left them no choice but to crowd into camps with farmers whose tame and settled lifestyle they previously despised. Bati, by some special irony, is the largest camp of all, a last resort for the hungry of much of Wollo. In it, nomads from the plains and peasants from the hills look exactly alike. Starvation is a great leveller.

The Rift is wide in the north, where it touches parts of four Ethiopian provinces: Eritrea, Tigre, Wollo and Harerghe. Towards the centre of the country, however, not far from the capital Addis Ababa, it narrows into a funnel, dividing the escarpment in two unequal parts. Into this channel are set Ethiopia's picturesque Rift Valley Lakes: Ziway, Abyata, Shala, Langano, Awasa, Abaya and Chamo.

Unlike the desert conditions of the Danakil Depression, this section of the Rift is fertile and relatively prosperous, its perennial lake system keeping it safe from the worst rigours of drought even in the bad years. Gazing on these lovely expanses of water today, one cannot help but speculate on the majesty that must once have been theirs when Africa was in its 'Pluvial' period, the great rains of prehistoric times that corresponded to the last northern European Ice Age. The lakes are, according to one geographer, 'but small puddles compared to their former size.' Nevertheless, their shrinkage has had positive consequences, exposing huge areas of alluvial soil to productive agriculture.

East of the Rift Valley Lakes stand the tall and misty peaks of the Bale mountains, a range that closely echoes the Simiens in its high-altitude ecology. Further east still, the land declines again into the plains of Harerghe. Here, across the endless red wastes of the savannah, Somali-speaking nomads, close relatives to the Afar, wander with their herds of camels and cattle following the sparse rains to transitory pastures. This is the 'Ogaden', a part of Ethiopia claimed by the neighbouring Somali Republic, which has been the scene of a number of bloody wars. Drought, too, is common here and, as a result of the failure of the 1984 long rains, some one million nomads are facing famine in the Ogaden in 1985.

To the west of the Rift Valley Lakes, one quickly finds oneself back in 'traditional' Ethiopia: terraced hillsides, regular fields, orderly villages of wattle-and-daub huts with conical thatched roofs. Here, in the provinces of Kaffa and Wollega, and in the southern parts of Shoa, some of the country's most productive farmlands are to be found and the spectre of drought seems distant and unreal. That this is so has little to do with environment and much to do with history for—in sharp contrast to Gonder, Eritrea, Tigre and Wollo, which have been farmed for thousands of years—the southern and western provinces are relatively recently settled, bear a light burden of population and have not been subjected to intensive and unplanned cultivation.

Kaffa is the centre of Ethiopia's coffee-growing industry (the country's largest foreign-exchange earner), and provides ideal conditions for the successful exploitation of the plant. Its rolling hillsides and valleys, at altitudes from 2,000 metres down to 1,300 metres, receive just the right amount of rainfall—1,500 to 2,000 millimetres a year—and have slightly acidic topsoils with pH values between 4.5 and 5.5, just right for high quality *Arabicas*.

Unfortunately, coffee does not feed people and, despite production increases, the purchasing power of Ethiopia's annual coffee crop has been steadily eroded over the last decade by deteriorating international terms of trade. The country's continuing need for foreign exchange to pay for its imports is certain to mean that ever greater acreages of the good land of Kaffa will be devoted to coffee and other cash crops in the future. It is to be hoped, however, that the government will be prepared to allocate at least equally large areas to food production.

Certainly the potential is there, for much of Kaffa is as yet completely unfarmed. The same is true of the neighbouring provinces of Wollega and Illubabor which consist substantially of wild, virgin lands. When I first travelled in these regions, accustomed as I was to the highly-populated north, it took me some time to get used to the silences, to the panoramic views uncluttered by roads, and, over vast areas, the near-complete absence of people. Another surprising sight was the presence of green forests that, in places, rolled over the land as far as the eye could see. This contrasted pleasantly with the picked-bald look of the north where shortage of firewood has been an issue for centuries and where deforestation has contributed significantly to the severity of the current drought.

Passing from Wollega to Illubabor on one of my journeys, I wrote:

The first main town of Illubabor is Metu, surrounded by singing forests filled with brightly-plumed birds. The mood here is that of a frontier settlement, the frontier being not a political one but rather the intangible borderline between raw nature and the endeavours of man. Ethiopia's Oromo people, who number more than half of the whole population of the country, and who have committed themselves to pushing this frontier back in their steady westwards expansion, crowd into Metu on holidays and weekends, drinking and listening to music in its many small bars, or offering their produce for sale in its outdoor market—produce that includes berries and wild honey as well as grains and vegetables. At night a small generator chugs and puffs bravely for an hour or two before it is closed down, and then darkness and silence together fall over the town like a veil.

The great asset of so much of western Ethiopia is this very frontier-like quality of as yet unexploited and unused potential. In the country as a whole, only *14 per cent* of the estimated 79 million hectares of good arable land is in fact under the plough. And out of a further three million hectares of land which could become productive if irrigated only 100,000 hectares are currently being exploited.

It does not take a major leap of the imagination to realize that in the green and fertile western territories there may lie some hope of salvation for the starving people of the grey and barren north. This is certainly the view of the government of Ethiopia, which, for some years, has been pursuing a low-key policy of resettlement at various points in Wollega, Kaffa and Illubabor. With the 1984 drought, this programme went into much higher gear and it now seems probable that as many as one and a half million people, mainly from Tigre and Wollo, will be resettled. Inevitably, migration on such a historic scale has implications that extend far beyond the limited scenarios of productivity and land-utilization sketched out by the economic planners and will, indeed, have a profound impact on the entire social and cultural fabric of modern Ethiopia.

Travelling westwards from Metu through Illubabor, one becomes conscious of a gradual change in the air and, by the time Gore, the regional capital, is reached it is obvious that the highlands are once again being left behind. It is here that the Ethiopian central massif, at its western extremity, quite suddenly comes to an end, dropping abruptly away towards the red and barren plains of the Sudan. Here, too, the highland peoples, ever reluctant to venture down into the burning deserts that surround them on all sides, have established a market where they can do business with the plains dwellers, tall Nuer and Anuak cattle herders, their faces and bodies scarred with elaborate tribal runes, speaking Nilotic languages totally unrelated to the Amharic and Oromo tongues that dominate much of the rest of Ethiopia.

The road leading westwards out of Gore, tripping off the escarpment and tumbling downwards through a long series of hairpin bends, takes the traveller into yet another of Ethiopia's many worlds. Far removed from the atmosphere of serious endeavour that permeates the highlands, the mood here in the far west is relaxed, slow and timeless. Despite the obvious fertility of the fields around the main river (the Baro, a tributary of the White Nile), the twin scourges of tsetse fly and malaria have restricted economic activity, with the result that population pressure is small. There are few signs of the modern world and the gentle, charming inhabitants of the region have an appealing innocence.

One of the most remarkable qualities of Ethiopia is the fact that it contains within one political boundary so much human and geographical diversity. The pagan Nilotic of the western plains, the learned Christian priest of the north studying his

Coptic bible, the lean, ascetic Muslim praying in an eastern mosque, the nomadic herdsmen of the lowlands, the parsimonious farmers of the high plateau, all are different facets of a country in which divergent themes of contrast and sudden transition combine to form a whole that is in every way greater than the sum of its parts.

Ethiopia's history is as varied and tumultuous as its landscapes and cultures. The first written records date back some 5,000 years and are found in the accounts of traders and travellers from Persia and Egypt, two of the first centres of human civilization. Such ancient contacts provide the background to the rise, more than three millennia ago, of the pre-Axumite and Axumite civilizations located in what are now the northern Ethiopian provinces of Eritrea and Tigre. Based on the city of Axum and the Red Sea port of Adulis (about 60 kilometres to the south of the modern port of Massawa) this powerful realm soon enjoyed close trading relations with Egypt, as well as with Arabia and India.

Of the glory that was Axum, little is immediately apparent today in the small Tigrean town of that name. Yet a closer look reveals that the modern dwellings perch above a vast part-buried, part-exposed archaeological site of incredible richness. Everywhere, the bones of long-gone eras protrude through the soil, adding substance to legends and bearing witness to lost truths embedded in myths and fable.

Axum's most famous daughter was Makeda, the legendary Queen of Sheba, who journeyed from here to visit King Solomon in Jerusalem and there, according to the first Book of Kings, 'communed with him of all that was in her heart.' The result of this communion was a son, Menelik I, who grew up in Ethiopia but travelled to Jerusalem as a young man where he spent several years before coming back to his own country with the fabled Ark of the Covenant which he and his companions had taken from the Temple.

The whole story of Solomon and Sheba, of course, straddles the misty boundary between history and myth, and Axum's claim to have been Sheba's capital is contested by a number of other cities in the Red Sea region. Many Ethiopians, however, take the tale at face value and it is still recounted as gospel by the superstitious peasants of the north. Wandering amongst the crumbling ruins of the once-great building on the outskirts of

Axum that is said to have been Sheba's castle, it is not difficult to tune in to the atmosphere of numinous dread on which Ethiopia's rulers over the centuries have played to enhance the prestige of their names. Haile Selassie in particular, the last Emperor, made much of his links to the Solomonic line, of which he claimed to be the 225th monarch. It is a telling measure of the forces unleashed by the Ethiopian revolution that, in 1974, it managed to break not only the material but also the spiritual basis of the Emperor's power and transform him overnight from a demigod into a clown.

Axum's best known archaeological relics are the stelae, pinnacles of solid granite, the tallest of which still standing tops 23 metres in height. But the city also houses the ruins of several fabulous palaces and of the oldest Christian church south of the Sahara, St Mary of Zion. In a chapel built near the exposed foundations of this church a shrouded object that Ethiopians believe to be the Ark of the Covenant is kept, guarded by stern-faced monks.

Regrettably, despite its rich archaeological heritage, very little excavation work has been possible in Axum for many years. This part of the province of Tigre suffers from profound political instability and has been the scene of much bitter fighting between government troops and rebel forces grouped together under the banner of the Tigre People's Liberation Front (TPLF). Aircraft flying into Axum, civilian as well as military, may not make the normal long, low approach but must rather spiral down in tight circles over the town to avoid machine-gun fire from the surrounding hills.

The TPLF, which does not confine itself to Tigre, has also been active in another important historical centre, Lalibela in neighbouring Wollo. Indeed, at the height of the 1984 drought, during the month of October, Lalibela was temporarily occupied by the TPLF and a number of tourists and aid-workers were kidnapped amidst maximum publicity.

Lalibela is famous for its imposing rock-hewn churches, often referred to as the eighth wonder of the world. These remarkable edifices, carved by hand from the mountainside on which Lalibela is built, date back to the early years of the 12th century, a period that saw the decline of Axum as a centre of Ethiopian civilization.

Lalibela's own period of prominence, however, was short-lived and, by the middle of the 13th century, the centre of power had again shifted south, this time to Shoa, where a medieval monarchy was established displaying many of the features associated with European feudalism, including a strong aristocracy and a close relationship between Church and State. There was no permanent capital, but rather a series of shifting military camps.

For Europeans of the time, this medieval Christian State in the heart of Ethiopia appeared as a land of mystery. It was often spoken of in wonder as the fabulous country of Prester John, the only Christian realm in Africa or Asia and, in the era of the Crusades, a potentially powerful ally of European Christendom in its conflict with Islam.

This conflict, long a factor in Ethiopian politics, took concrete form in the 16th century when one Ahmed Ibn Ibrahim El Ghazi, nicknamed *Gragn* (meaning 'left-handed'), launched a holy war from the east. After several years of fighting, the Christian emperor defeated Gragn with the help of troops sent from Portugal; however, much damage had been done.

For Ethiopia, one positive consequence of Gragn's war was the shift of the capital, away from the fighting, to the north-west in the region of Lake Tana. Here, in 1636, Emperor Fasilidas founded the city of Gonder which became the site of many stately castles and palaces, most of which still stand to this day. The emperors who held court at Gonder were, however, unable to reconquer the territories lost in the early part of Gragn's invasion and later, in the 18th century, faced virtually insuperable political and military difficulties as the central power of the state collapsed. The country entered a period of disintegration and civil war which Ethiopian historians termed the era of *masfent*, or 'judges', for it resembled the period of the Old Testament judges when 'there was no king in Israel; every man did what was right in his own eyes.'

The 19th century thus dawned on a divided Ethiopia in which there was no central authority and in which the governors of the principal provinces, though still nominally subject to an Emperor at Gonder, were in fact virtually independent and fought against each other as and when they pleased. Analysing this period, the leading historian of Ethiopia, Dr Richard Pankhurst, nevertheless concludes that 'most of the provinces continued to share a common culture. Memories of the country's great and glorious past were, moreover, never forgotten. Many people yearned for the return of peace and prosperity. Several of the more far-sighted realised that this could in fact only be achieved through technical progress.'

A number of 19th-century emperors, notably Tewodros II and Yohannes IV, did take significant steps in the direction of modernization and reunification; however, their efforts were overshadowed by those of Emperor Menelik II (1889–1913), who was responsible for the reintegration of the lost provinces of the south as well as for bringing Ethiopia into the 20th century.

Menelik laid the foundations of the modern Ethiopian state, founded the capital Addis Ababa, and introduced technical innovations including the first railway, the first paved roads, the first motor car, the first modern schools and hospitals, the first printing press, and the first postage stamps. Perhaps his greatest achievement, however, was that he defeated an Italian invasion at the battle of Adwa in Tigre province in 1896, 'the most notable victory,' as Dr Pankhurst puts it, 'of an African over a European army since the time of Hannibal.' In winning this battle, Menelik succeeded in establishing his country's independence during the period of the 'scramble for Africa' when the European colonial powers were carving up the continent amongst themselves.

The Italians did, however, manage to hold on to their original conquest, the coastal province of Eritrea, subsequently used by Mussolini as a bridgehead from which to launch a second—and this time successful—invasion of Ethiopia in 1935, some 22 years after Menelik's death. The Italian occupation—it can in no sense be considered a colonization—lasted for six years, hotly opposed throughout by Ethiopian partisans. It was finally brought to an end by the intervention of the Allied forces in 1941, and Emperor Haile Selassie, who had been in exile throughout the occupation in the relative comfort of the English city of Bath, was reinstalled on the throne.

In the post-war years, Haile Selassie (the name means 'Power of the Trinity') made a number of efforts to continue the trend of modernization that had been started at the turn of the century by Menelik. He was quickly to find, however, that modernization was a tiger: riding on its back he was safe; but, when he tried to get off, it turned around and ate him.

CHAPTER TWO

The Emperor and the Revolution

Haile Selassie was crowned Emperor of Ethiopia in November 1930 at a ceremony in Addis Ababa's Cathedral attended by representatives of all the great powers and by a splendid array of journalists. Five years later the Italian invasion sent the Lion of Judah into genteel exile in England from which he returned with the Allies in 1941.

A self-styled modernizer, Selassie presided over, and drew his power from, what was essentially a feudal domain. The contradictions were evident from the start. For example, the 1955 Constitution that he pushed through with the stated intention of encouraging 'the modern Ethiopian to accustom himself to take part in the direction of all departments of the State,' and 'to share in the mighty task which Ethiopian Sovereigns have had to accomplish alone in the past,' contained the following wording:

> The Imperial dignity shall remain perpetually attached to the line of Haile Selassie I, whose Line descends without interruption from the dynasty of Menelik I, son of the Queen of Ethiopia, the Queen of Sheba, and King Solomon of Jerusalem. . . . By virtue of His Imperial Blood, as well as by the anointing which He has received, the Person of the Emperor is sacred, His Dignity inviolable and His Power indisputable. . . .

The capital letters say it all. Here was a man who wanted to enjoy the reputation of an enlightened reformer without having to pay the price of his reforms. This was particularly evident in his toleration of the age-old system of land tenure in which absentee landlords skimmed off anything from 50 to 75 per cent of the produce of the disenfranchised peasants who worked their fields. Indeed, under the guise of democratization, Haile Selassie not only tolerated this system but also extended and complicated it. Members of the country's emerging middle class (a potential threat to imperial power) were given land grants that encouraged them to identify their interests with those of the aristocracy; at the same time, newly-devised government taxes further impoverished and embittered the peasants.

These trends had their most severe implications in the southern provinces reintegrated into the Ethiopian empire by Menelik II. The feudal tradition, so strong in the north, had no deep historical roots in the south where the land, until the end of the 19th century, was largely divided up into smallholdings owned by the peasants who farmed them. Under Haile Selassie this egalitarian situation came to an end. Two-thirds of the land was confiscated by the state and then handed over to local warlords (*Rases*) as a reward for supporting imperial policy. These warlords in turn were encouraged to subdivide their allotted territory amongst their retainers who became landlords in their own right. According to Ethiopian historian and analyst Berket Habte Selassie, it was not unusual for a great feudal lord in Haile Selassie's empire to be given the ownership of whole provinces: Ras Birru, for instance, owned most of Arssi and a substantial slice of Harerghe. 'The undistributed part of the confiscated land remained in the state's domain,' Berket tells us, 'and grants from it continued to be made until the revolution of 1974. Indeed, this was one of the most important ways in which Haile Selassie was able to buy off the emergent bourgeoisie.'

That the Emperor stayed in power as long as he did was a result of more than mere material manipulation. There was also a profound reluctance amongst the general populace to oppose him. The mystical language of the Constitution, enshrining his divine right to rule, hints at the whole substratum of Ethiopian superstitions and magical beliefs on which he was able to draw to maintain the status quo. And despite his own rationalist Western education, there is ample evidence that the Emperor himself was deeply enmeshed in magical practices. It is still whispered by retainers who were close to him that, in the latter part of his rule, he indulged in human sacrifice. Fearing old age, and believing that a demon who wished him to grow old and frail resided in one of the crater lakes at Debre Zeit, the Emperor arranged for a virgin girl to be sacrificed each December on the anniversary of his birthday. The victim's blood was distributed on the waters of the lake to appease the demon and then the Emperor went in to bathe.

Nevertheless, for all that was dark and medieval in his rule, Haile Selassie did bring changes to Ethiopia, and it was these changes that destroyed him. Most notably, he created a higher education system which, by functioning properly, produced students with questioning, critical minds. When the Emperor tried to put a stop to their criticisms and gag their questions they rose up against him. He created a small but vigorous industrial sector and, within it, the nucleus of a radical working class complete with trade unions—that were soon to bring Addis Ababa to a halt in a series of strikes. He created a well organized modern army which, while enhancing his prestige, also had the potential to remove him from his throne—a potential that was finally realized in September 1974.

In an Ethiopia that was gradually awakening from the slumber of ages, it was extremely unlikely that Haile Selassie could have survived the 1970s even if everything had been going well in his empire.

Everything was not going well, however.

A sustained drought, combined with the inefficiency of the feudal system of agriculture, had produced conditions of severe famine in the provinces of Wollo and Tigre that, at a conservative estimate, killed 200,000 people between 1972 and 1974. The imperial government did nothing at all to alleviate the effects of this famine, or to succour its victims. On the contrary a concerted effort was made to hush the whole thing up with the result that no international or, for that matter, national aid-giving effort was launched until it was much too late. It took a foreigner, TV producer Jonathan Dimbleby, to capture on film the horrific images of death and destitution, and to contrast them in a direct way with the great wealth, the pomp, and the prodigious banquets of the Emperor's court.

It was a curious irony of modern mass communication that Ethiopians in Addis Ababa thus learned about the starvation that was taking place in provinces just a few hundred kilometres to their north by means of second-hand information from those of their compatriots who had seen Dimbleby's film in Europe and America. As this information began to filter back, however, the local reaction was swift and to the point with numerous efforts being made at all levels of the community to raise funds and food supplies for the famine victims.

The imperial government, which still took no effective action, came to be seen as corrupt and inept. For some months, however, it seemed that no specific blame was going to be attached to the holy name of the Emperor. Rather, in the 'creeping coup' that slowly gathered momentum during 1974, it was the Emperor's advisers who came under attack and who, one by one, were pruned away from him, jailed and executed.

The 'pruning' was done under the direction of a body of junior army officers who called themselves the *Dergue* (the word means 'committee' in Amharic) and who at all times, right up to the end, claimed to be acting in the name of the Emperor. The end came on 12 September 1974, the second day of the Ethiopian New Year, when Haile Selassie was arrested at his palace. A little less than a year later, an insignificant notice appeared in Addis Ababa's daily newspaper announcing his death.

The end for the Emperor was, however, just the end of the beginning for Ethiopia's revolution which was soon to be hailed by communists and fellow travellers worldwide as 'the only genuine revolution in Africa'.

The *Dergue*, which had ushered the revolution in, was, by nature, a formless, disorganized body at first uncertain of its own purpose or direction. However, it did contain within its ranks one formative, highly organized and committed personality—an ordnance officer, Lt Col. Mengistu Haile Mariam. By the beginning of 1977, and after much bloodletting, Mengistu emerged as the undisputed leader of the revolution, a position which he occupies to this day.

The Ethiopian revolution has much about it that is attractive, and much that is unattractive.

On the negative side must be counted the era of the 'Red Terror and the White Terror', a period of turmoil in 1977 and 1978 when the *Dergue* struggled with 'counter-revolutionary elements' in the streets of Addis Ababa and thousands of people, often themselves young radicals, perished. The families of those executed were obliged to pay for the bullets that had killed their relatives, and displays of grief were forbidden. The principal instruments of this campaign were the *kebeles* (neighbourhood associations) of which there are more than 500 in Addis Ababa, each with a membership of approximately 3,000. Within the *kebeles* witch-hunts of suspected opponents of the regime were common and the techniques of 'confession' and 'self-criticism' were employed with a zeal reminiscent of the Spanish Inquisition.

Press coverage of this turbulent period did much to condition the unfavourable image of the Ethiopian revolution that still prevails in the West. Ethiopian radicals, however, regard the Red Terror/White Terror as their baptism of fire, a collective experience through which the country had to pass if it was to forge itself anew.

Another negative aspect of the revolution, perhaps because of its military origins, is that it has promoted an extremely structured and hierarchical administrative system which discourages individual initiative. There is an over-reliance in decision-making on directives from the top and, in the absence of such directives, committees are formed which are often very slow to take action. The result is an extremely slow-moving, timid and unimaginative bureaucracy which has, on a number of occasions, failed to come to grips decisively with pressing development problems.

On the credit side of the balance sheet, solid progress has been made in a number of areas since 1974.

One of the first priorities after Haile Selassie was overthrown was the implementation of a sweeping land-reform programme. This programme, begun in 1975, has since come to be regarded as one of the most successful of its kind in the world. All land was nationalized at a stroke, with private holdings subsequently being limited to 10 hectares. This effectively did away with landlords and the entire feudal system of production and, while it did not guarantee greater output, it has at least ensured that the national cake is more fairly shared.

There is no doubt that the major beneficiaries of this programme have been the millions of landless peasants in the southern provinces upon whose labour Haile Selassie's particular brand of imperial feudalism was based. The redistribution has meant that their lot in life has been significantly improved and, inevitably, the revolution counts its staunchest supporters amongst them. The challenge for the future, however, is to take land reform beyond simple redistribution into increased productivity—a goal that has so far not been achieved, with large parts of the agricultural sector stagnant over the last 10 years.

Co-operatives and state farms are the instruments that have been selected to develop agriculture and, through them, bank credits and other incentives have been made available to communities that previously were unable to raise the capital to buy modern tools and equipment. At the same time, however, many observers are critical of Ethiopia's collectivized-farming approach which has failed to show results in terms of output. The government's policy of paying low prices for food crops is identified as another factor in the poor performance of the sector since it acts as a disincentive to increased production. Clearly, much remains to be done and this is an area in which long-term aid and technical assistance from Western governments could make a significant contribution if granted with good will and on a large enough scale.

Parallel to the land reform programme, urban reform was also instituted limiting home ownership to one house per family. This again has had positive effects, particularly in overcrowded cities like Addis Ababa where shortage of accommodation for the poor has traditionally been a severe problem. Inevitably also, at the same time as land reform and urban reform, all industries were nationalized—although this latter measure has had a less profound impact on Ethiopian society since industrial workers constitute only a tiny proportion of the total population.

The redistributive ethic of the revolution has not been confined to property ownership and the means of production. In the cultural sphere it has been applied most notably to Ethiopia's education system—the benefits of which were, under Haile Selassie, strictly limited to the aristocracy and the emerging middle class. Between 1974 and 1984 the number of elementary and secondary school children in the country was increased from one million to three million, the number of school age children attending school from 19 per cent to 49 per cent, and the number of teachers from 24,800 to 54,886. Perhaps the most important progress, however, has been made in the field of adult literacy. The National Literacy Campaign has reduced the number of adults unable to read and write from 93 per cent to 37 per cent through the mechanism of more than 300 literacy centres in all parts of the country. So effective has this campaign been that it is widely regarded as a model of its kind and has received a major UNESCO award.

Because of its many real achievements, the Ethiopian revolution has received accolades from a number of very different quarters. In 1977, for example, Fidel Castro wrote this paean of revolutionary praise:

> In Ethiopia they have adopted very radical measures. In a feudal country, where the peasants were slaves, they nationalized the land and distributed it among the peasants. They carried out an urban reform, allowing only one house to a family. They organized a powerful movement in the cities, a form of organization they called the *kebele*. That is, they organized the families in the poor urban areas. They nationalized the principal industries of the country, revolutionized the armed forces, politicized the soldiers, created Political Committees.

In the same year a right-wing British organization, the Institute of Conflict Studies, reported in its journal: '. . . . the *Dergue* can point to success in having broken most of the ties of feudal interdependency that dominated personal relations in Ethiopia and which many observers felt would constitute the greatest obstacle on the road to modernity.'

Winning praise from both Castro and the Institute of Conflict Studies could be said to be an achievement in itself. Much more important than this kind of widespread recognition, however, is the simple fact that, in its first decade, the regime managed to bring the country intact through a period of great social turmoil, at the same time moving towards a gradual democratization of the institutions of its rule. Most observers agree that in conditions which elsewhere would have promoted the growth of a self-serving military tyranny, the armed forces in Ethiopia have gradually loosened their hold on the reins of power—a process that reached a watershed of sorts in 1984 with the establishment of the Workers' Party of Ethiopia. While there are grounds for being cynical about the WPE's credentials, the fact is that it is there and that its structure holds forth at least the possibility of broadly-based participation in government.

An effective foreign policy must also be counted amongst the achievements of the Ethiopian revolution. Despite the radical rhetoric of the regime, constantly punctuated with tirades against 'imperialism' and 'international capitalism', Ethiopia in the 1980s has shown a great deal of pragmatism and common sense in its international relations, and this suggests that an intelligent and careful evaluation of the national interest ultimately carries more weight than ideology. A good illustration of this, in the troubled and unstable Horn of Africa, is to be found in the close and friendly ties that Ethiopia enjoys with Kenya to the south and Djibouti to the east, both countries that are unashamedly 'capitalist' and free-enterprise-oriented in their own domestic political and economic affairs. At the same time, at the other end of the political spectrum, Ethiopia is on very good terms with Libya and with the People's Democratic Republic of Yemen, both of which can only be regarded as extreme radicals. Ethiopia's ability to make and sustain such an eclectic range of friendships while at the same time refusing to compromise or warp its own internal policies in any way is a sign of quite masterful statesmanship.

All in all, therefore, and cutting a long story very short indeed, I believe it is fair to say that the government of Ethiopia in the mid 1980s has emerged as a mature and responsible member of the community of nations. More than this, it can be said to have implemented domestic policies that have, by and large, benefited the majority of Ethiopians. It would be quite wrong to conclude from this evaluation, however, that Ethiopia's problems are over since, as the tragedy of the 1984 famine has indicated, the contrary is true.

Bad famines, unlike good marriages, are not made in heaven. All the evidence suggests that disasters of this kind are usually produced by Acts of Man, not Acts of God. Ethiopia is no exception to this rule.

The particular Act of Man that has had at least as much to do with the severity of the current famine as the failure of the rains is referred to within Ethiopia as 'the regional problem', a neat euphemism that disguises an extremely complicated social and political mess which the country must solve if it is ever to realize its full potential for progress and development.

Ethiopia is a country of many 'nationalities', a diverse, heterogeneous amalgam of peoples tied to one another by history and by geographical proximity. There are more than 80 different language groups and an almost equally great variety of lifestyles. Even religion, often a unifying factor, is here potentially divisive:

Christianity and Islam, each claiming about 40 per cent of the population, have been in competition for the souls of Ethiopians since the seventh century; various brands of paganism and animism also hold sway in much of the south and west of the country.

The imposition of the structure of a modern nation state, one professing Marxism-Leninism at that, on top of so complex and turbulent a mixture, could not be expected to take place without upheavals of one kind or another and Ethiopia has had more than its fair share of such upheavals since 1974.

Just three years after the revolution, the *Dergue* found itself facing insurrection in no less than 12 of the country's 14 provinces. The two most serious of these rebellions were in Eritrea, in the north, and in the Ogaden, an eastern region, colloquially named after one of the nomadic Somali-speaking tribes living there, which spreads over much of the provinces of Harerghe, Bale and Sidamo.

The Somali revolt, beefed up by a full-scale invasion from the neighbouring Somali Republic, seemed set fair to bring down the Ethiopian government; the resulting Ogaden war of 1977–78 became the hottest armed conflict going on anywhere in the world at that time. By 1984, however, the problem posed by the irredentism of Ethiopia's Somali-speaking peoples had died down to such an extent that the Ogaden was a secure area, through which travellers could pass freely, and the site for a number of major development projects.

The same, sadly, cannot be said of Eritrea which, along with the neighbouring province of Tigre, and contiguous parts of Wollo and Gonder, today constitutes a vast landscape of instability and lingering violence where the main human activity is war. It is no coincidence that it is also this precise area which has been most seriously affected during the 1984–85 famine.

The Eritrea and Tigre problems, although now linked in a number of important ways, have distinct historical roots. The former antedates the revolution by many years; the latter is recent, with the first shots fired in 1975. Both, however, have been catalysed by the turmoil that Ethiopia as a whole was thrown into after 1974.

Eritrea is Ethiopia's northernmost province, occupying a long wedge of land with an area of some 100,000 square kilometres bounded to the north by the Red Sea, to the north west by the Republic of Sudan and to the south east by the Republic of Djibouti. Its strategic and economic significance lies in the fact that it contains Ethiopia's only ports, Massawa and Assab (although Assab has, for the last several years, been treated as a separate administrative region).

Like the rest of Ethiopia, Eritrea is characterized by contrasting landscapes, cultures and religions. The province contains several distinct ethnic/linguistic groups: about half the population of three million is made up of Christian Tigrinya speakers; the balance, largely Muslims, speak Tigre, Arabic, Saho, Afar and other tongues.

The Muslims, as again is the case elsewhere in the country, occupy the low ground; the highlanders are Christians. I remember noticing, when I first drove from the port of Massawa to the city of Asmara, Eritrea's regional capital, how clear-cut and obvious this divide was: on the coastal plains mosques and veiled women; three hours' drive away churches and girls in tight jeans; in between the two a dusty road rising out of the desert to wind perilously up the face of the escarpment.

Another thing that I could not help noticing as I made that journey, and which gave an even more fundamental clue to the nature of Eritrea today, was the debris of warfare stacked up alongside the road: here a T-54 tank, the victim of a wire-guided missile, its turret blown off, there a burnt-out APC, and there a rusting artillery piece, its muzzle pointing at the sky. Massawa itself is scarred and pockmarked with bullet holes and craters. On nearby Gurgusum beach, countless shell-cases litter the sands, and once-fashionable villas and beach houses lean drunkenly, their roofs and walls blown in.

The war that left these signs, and that still goes on today (though its epicentre has moved away from the Massawa-Asmara corridor), has the sorry distinction of being Africa's longest-running conflict. Nowhere else in a continent renowned for its lost causes has so much courage, ingenuity and effort, not to say human blood, been so consistently expended to so little avail.

Supporters of Eritrean independence, and supporters of the nationalist stand of the Ethiopian government, can both find a fair amount of historical justification for their respective views. The former point to the several periods when Eritrea, or parts of Eritrea, were administered separately from the rest of

Ethiopia; the latter argue that the Eritrean highlands, together
with the province of Tigre, were at the very heart of the ancient
Axumite kingdom out of which all subsequent Ethiopian
states were born. Both parties, as authors Fred Halliday and
Maxine Molyneux point out in their study of the Ethiopian
revolution, make the conventional assumption that in previous
centuries

> entities corresponding to 'Ethiopia' or 'Eritrea' existed. This
> ignores the fact that all nations are historically formed. In
> reality, no distinct and united area corresponding to Eritrea
> was at any time an independent entity in the pre-colonial
> period. An Ethiopian entity did exist, but the extent and centre
> of the Christian kingdoms of the interior varied considerably
> over the centuries. In other words, neither 'Eritrea' nor 'Ethi-
> opia' as presently constituted existed in the pre-colonial
> period. The ambiguous links between 'Eritrea' and the rest
> of today's Ethiopia must be seen in the light of this ebb and
> flow, which, variously interpreted, provides both a precedent
> and a reserve of retrospective legitimation for the conflicts that
> were to come.

When Emperor Menelik II defeated the Italians on the Tigrean
battlefield of Adwa in 1896 he prevented the colonization of
Ethiopia. However the Italians kept their foothold in Eritrea,
their first conquest on the Ethiopian mainland, and here they
did create a colony. Forty-five years of Italian rule did much to
create a separate Eritrean consciousness and when the Italians
were defeated in 1941 during the turmoil of World War II, there
were groups within Eritrea determined to maintain an identity
separate from that of Ethiopia.

In the immediate post-war years, the issue of what was to
happen to Eritrea became something of an international *cause
célèbre* with Haile Selassie's Ethiopia, the British, the Italians, the
French, the Americans, the Russians, and the nascent Arab
nationalist movements in Egypt and elsewhere all taking an
interest. A Commission of the Four Great Powers made a
fact-finding tour of the area in 1947 but could not agree on the
facts that were found. While the commissioners from Britain
and America produced evidence that 71 per cent of the highland
population desired to return to Ethiopia, the commissioners

of the USSR and France came out in favour of a trusteeship administration under Italy.

In the end, after further commissions, and much deliberation in the General Assembly of the United Nations, the decision was taken that Eritrea should be federated with Ethiopia. The Resolution to this effect, adopted by the General Assembly on 2 December 1950, stated that it took into consideration:

(a) the wishes and the welfare of the inhabitants of Eritrea, including the views of the various racial, religious and political groups of the provinces of the territory and the capacity of the people for self-government; (b) the interests of peace and security in East Africa; (c) the rights and claims of Ethiopia based on geographical, historical, ethnic, or economic reasons, including, in particular, Ethiopia's legitimate need for access to the sea. . . .

Further, it was the hope of the General Assembly that the federation would assure to the inhabitants of Eritrea 'the fullest respect and safeguards for their institutions, traditions, religions, and languages, as well as the widest possible measure of self government.'

As the UN envisaged it, Eritrea was to have an 'autonomous government' with fairly complete control over its internal affairs, but with external affairs including trade and defence to be under federal jurisdiction. From the first days of the inception of the federation in 1952, however, with 15 local political parties competing in the elections for the Eritrean Assembly (on platforms as different as total independence for Eritrea on the one hand and complete union with Ethiopia on the other) the prospects for this attractive vision looked bleak. A further complicating factor was Emperor Haile Selassie's obvious determination to ensure that his writ ran in Eritrea every bit as strongly as it did elsewhere in the country. Accordingly, leaders of the separatist factions were subjected to increasing harassment as the 1950s wore on. This in turn strengthened Eritrean opposition to what came to be seen as Ethiopian interference in the internal affairs of the province and, by the middle of the decade, the Assembly was passing frequent resolutions accusing the Emperor of violating political and civil rights. The Emperor's response was characteristically harsh: political parties were banned, outspoken

newspapers closed down, trade unions broken. By 1962 the
federal identity of Eritrea was *de facto* a thing of the past; no one
was surprised when the Assembly, dominated by the Emperor's
men, decided to cement this state of affairs *de jure* by formally
dissolving all federal institutions and integrating the province
fully into Ethiopia.

It was then, in September 1962, that the war in Eritrea began.
Out of the Pandora's box of the dissolved federation a swarm
of liberation movements rose up to plague Ethiopia. Quarrelling
amongst themselves, many of these movements were also
characterized by serious internal rifts. One of the earliest established, for example, the Eritrean Liberation Front (ELF), split
down the middle in 1970 to form two new groups, the ELF-
Revolutionary Command and the ELF-Popular Liberation
Forces. This latter group changed its name in 1971 to the
Eritrean Popular Liberation Forces, before dividing again in 1976
into the ELF-PLF on the one hand and the Eritrean Popular
Liberation Front on the other.

Out of this complicated and dangerous game of musical acro-
nyms there finally emerged, from 1976 onwards, three major
fronts: the original ELF, the newly renamed EPLF, and the
ELF-PLF. Their greatest strength, beyond their evident appeal
to different sections of the Eritrean population, lay in the external
support that each received from the neighbouring Republic of
Sudan, support in the form of an open border, safe refuge in
military camps beyond the reach of Ethiopian hot pursuit, and
guaranteed supply lines. Their greatest weakness was that they
were frequently as bitterly opposed to one another as they were
to their common enemy.

The Ethiopian revolution of 1974, by throwing the country
into turmoil, created a golden opportunity for the various
Eritrean secession movements. Taking advantage of the dis-
array of the central government and, particularly, of the huge
military diversion caused by the Ogaden war in 1977, the three
fronts were able, by early 1978, to claim control of most of
Eritrea. Almost all the countryside was theirs, as well as all
the major towns with the exception of Asmara, which was
surrounded, and Massawa, which was under siege.

This was the time, if there ever was a suitable season for
it, when a provincial Eritrean government might have been
established thus consolidating the military victories in the politi-

cal and diplomatic spheres. The Eritreans, however, threw away the chance that circumstances had thrown at them by choosing this moment to escalate what was already virtually a civil war amongst themselves. They paid for the luxury of their squabbling in a series of reversals that drove them back from the centre of the province to the badlands of the north-west where, despite some significant excursions, they have remained largely confined to this day.

One vital factor, which none of the Eritrean fronts could have predicted, was the overwhelming military support that Ethiopia was to receive during 1977–78 from its Eastern Bloc allies, particularly the Soviet Union and Cuba. Another important consideration, which the guerrillas evidently seriously underestimated, was the absolute determination of the Ethiopian government to rule in Eritrea.

There had been some speculation that the revolution would take a softer line on the issue of Eritrean secession than Haile Selassie had done, particularly since the ideology professed by the *Dergue* and the ideologies of the main Eritrean rebel groups were, at least on the face of things, identical. In the event, however, despite some early attempts at dialogue, the military rulers of revolutionary Ethiopia, nationalists at heart, turned out to be far more ruthless opponents of the Eritrean cause than the Emperor had ever been. This was particularly the case from 1977 onwards when the *Dergue* came under the chairmanship of Lt Col. Mengistu Haile Mariam, a man who has since frequently demonstrated himself to be committed above all else to the twin ideals of strong leadership and an undivided Ethiopia.

In a keynote speech in June 1978, Mengistu summed up government policy: 'The primary objective of the . . . war is to affirm Ethiopia's historical unity, and to safeguard her outlet to the sea, and to defend her very existence from being stifled.' While the historical argument is open to some debate, it is easy to see and sympathize with Ethiopia's point of view in wishing to ensure that its access to the sea is not blocked by the emergence of a hostile Eritrean state. Similarly, given the multi-ethnic nature of Ethiopia, it is obvious that Eritrean secession, if it were allowed, would set precedents which might lead to total anarchy and, in the place of Ethiopia as we know it, the emergence of a series of antagonistic mini-nations—here the Oromos, here the Somalis, here the Eritreans, here the Tigreans, here the Afars, and so on. What government, confronted by such a spectre, would not seek to put down provincial rebellions with the utmost firmness?

At the same time, it is also easy to sympathize with the Eritrean point of view—here, after all, are a brave and ingenious people so determined to exercise the universally recognized right of self-determination that they have been prepared to sacrifice their lives for it for the last 23 years. Why should they not have their independence, since that is what they so manifestly seem to desire?

Much the same time as Mengistu was making his speech in 1978, the EPLF issued a Memorandum on 'The Right of the Eritrean People to Self-Determination' in which it asserted: 'The Eritrean people must be free in order to prosper and advance in peace. The legitimacy of the question of Eritrean national independence is beyond argument because it has been occasioned by history and the record of bitter struggles.' This is a position which many observers, particularly Western intellectuals, find it difficult to disagree with, doubly so because of the social and economic achievements of the Eritrean guerrillas who, in their 'liberated areas' have created admirable health-care and education systems and a thriving underground economy. At the same time, however, if we are completely honest, it is a position which we in the West are reluctant to apply in our own countries where, for example, separatist movements in Northern Ireland and Spain get short shrift from the authorities. Surely it is unreasonable to expect the government of Ethiopia, immersed as it is in the harsh realities of Third World politics, to set an example that we in the industrialized countries are ourselves unprepared to follow?

So the debate goes on. But what for Western observers is a stirring philosophical argument on issues like human rights and self-determination is, for Eritreans and Ethiopians, a much more concrete matter of blood, death and destruction. The contest now approaching its silver jubilee and obliging the Ethiopian government to spend upwards of one million US dollars a day on 'defence' has, at a conservative estimate, cost a quarter of a million lives, created a million refugees, and, worst of all, diverted the resources and creativity of two great peoples from development activities into the non-productive pursuit of war. The tragedy is that this is a war that cannot be won by either side and that holds forth only the prospect of two increasingly weary and punch-drunk leviathans, the government and the guerrillas, endlessly bludgeoning each other amidst a bleak and wasted no-man's land of drought, pestilence and famine.

In the years since 1978 there have been a number of developments in the Eritrean conflict, notably the emergence of the Marxist EPLF as the dominant military force amongst the guerrillas with an armed militia estimated at 30,000 men. Nevertheless, the basic scenario has not changed. The Ethiopian Government, still very much under the leadership of Chairman Mengistu Haile Mariam, is still committed to nothing less than total defeat of Eritrean separatism. The Eritrean separatists, for their part, are still calling unequivocally for the total independence of their province.

The pragmatic problem remains, however, that any real hope of setting up an Eritrean state was lost after the guerrillas failed to take advantage of the uniquely favourable conditions prevailing in 1977–78. Therefore, as Halliday and Molyneux put it, 'the choice facing the Eritreans in the period after 1978 was not whether to exercise the right to secession but whether to continue to fight the Ethiopians indefinitely with no realistic expectation of victory. . . .' Regrettably, if understandably, this is the choice that the guerrillas have opted for. The people of Eritrea, and of Ethiopia's other 13 provinces, are today paying the price in a famine that could have been avoided, drought or no drought, had the country been at peace.

Immediately to the south of Eritrea, the province of Tigre is also in revolt. The uprising here, led by the Tigre People's Liberation Front, is more recent than that of Eritrea, but it is also potentially more destabilizing and it has contributed even more directly to the severity of the famine. An estimated 80 per cent of the province is outside the government's control with the result that most relief efforts simply do not get through. Small-scale programmes mounted by voluntary agencies like Oxfam and War on Want are underway behind TPLF lines but these, and the development activities of the guerrillas themselves, are so disrupted by the continuing fighting that they have had little impact.

Tigre consists largely of central highland plateau cut through with formidable valleys and sloping down in the east and west to low-lying plains. The majority language is Tigrinya, closely identified with the majority religion, Christianity, to which more than 70 per cent of the population adheres. Minority languages are Afar, Agew, Kunama and Saho, mainly spoken by lowland pastoralists who follow the Muslim faith.

Nine tenths of all Tigreans earn their living from the land with subsistence agriculture the dominant activity. Wheat, barley, millet, sorghum, maize, and *teff* (a grain indigenous to the Ethiopian plateau) are the main crops, but sesame, beans and cotton are also grown.

Tigre is probably the most intensively farmed of all Ethiopia's provinces with a tradition of settled agriculture that dates back for many thousands of years. The overused and deforested terrain is in places seriously eroded and the topsoils are thin and devoid of nutrients. As a result there have been five major famines here in the last 30 years and, according to one United Nations Environment Programme report, the continuing efforts of the Tigreans 'to scrape a bare living from this land threaten to destroy it completely.' Unless radical steps are taken, the simple fact is that Tigre has no future. War and imaginative development, however, make poor bedfellows.

The conflict in Tigre began in 1974–5 when an aristocrat, Ras Mengesha Seyoum, organized a Tigre Liberation Front to oppose the revolution. By 1976, however, the TLF itself had become radicalized with the influx into its ranks of many young, left-wing intellectuals. Under their influence the organization adopted a Maoist programme and renamed itself the Tigre People's Liberation Front. Shortly thereafter it began to accept training and logistical assistance from the EPLF in Eritrea with the result that, by 1978, it had emerged as a significant force with an armed militia thought to be about 10,000 strong.

In the 1980s, while avoiding pitched battles with government troops, the TPLF has pulled off a number of spectacular guerrilla raids including, in October 1984, the occupation of the historic city of Lalibela in neighbouring Wollo province. The Front's speciality from a public-relations point of view has been the kidnap of tourists and aid workers, all of whom have subsequently been released to tell tales of government oppression and guerrilla heroism.

Unlike the EPLF, the TPLF is not in essence a secessionist movement. In its own words, contained in a statement to the UN General Assembly in 1981, it is:

a people's democratic front fighting for the national self-determination of the Tigrean people and waging a people's democratic revolution. The TPLF is not fighting for secession. It is not against the *voluntary* unity of the five million Tigreans with other nations and nationalities in the empire state. The TPLF understands the economic, security and international advantages of a big state. It is only when there does not exist a democratic atmosphere, when their political rights are grossly violated, when they lead a degrading economic and social life, when the national oppression continues or is aggravated, i.e. when there do not exist the conditions for living with others, that the people opt for the formation of an independent and democratic republic.

In other words, what the TPLF is saying is that it seeks a reconstituted Ethiopia, in which all the nationalities have an effective voice. In the absence of any movement in this direction, however, it will struggle to pull Tigre out of Ethiopia.

Once again, particularly for the liberally-inclined Western intellectual, it is difficult not to feel some sympathy for the ultimate reasonableness of the TPLF's position. In practice, however, faced with the considerable might of the Ethiopian state, the TPLF, like the EPLF, is pursuing a lost cause and the best that it can hope to achieve is the situation that prevails at present—a bloody stalemate with neither government nor guerrillas fully in control and any hope of long-term development indefinitely prevented.

There would seem, therefore, particularly in context of the current famine, to be a *prima facie* case for saying that the time has come when the supporters of both the Eritrean and the Tigrean Fronts should press the guerrillas to seek a negotiated settlement with the Ethiopian government. The counter-argument to this, of course, is that it is the Ethiopian government that should be persuaded to negotiate. Someone, however, has to be first to break the vicious circle.

Africa is full of examples of bitter, apparently insoluble struggles, which have been resolved either through overwhelming force or through common sense and which have led on to constructive, creative relationships characterized by respect for human rights. Biafra, defeated in the Nigerian civil war amidst prophecies of genocide, is an illustration of the former case.

Southern Sudan, peacefully federated with northern Sudan in the early 1970s after a 20-year war, is an illustration of the latter, although that federation is today again under strain.

Significantly, Ethiopia itself contains a precedent which suggests that the worst fears of the EPLF and the TPLF would prove groundless were they to seek a negotiated solution with the central government. This precedent is that of the Somali peoples of eastern Ethiopia who, in the Ogaden war of 1977–78 saw themselves as the government's bitterest opponents. It was perhaps their good fortune that they were decisively defeated in that war, rather than put into a no-win no-lose position, because having accepted their defeat with commendable pragmatism, they have subsequently turned the post-war situation very much to their advantage. Several valuable development programmes are now underway in the Ogaden, refugees from across the border in Somalia and Djibouti are returning to their homes, and the general atmosphere of peace and stability in the region has helped to promote active commerce—all of which goes to confirm that the Somalis have managed to extract the maximum in economic, social and political concessions from a government anxious to prove its magnanimity. As the leader of one of the largest Somali groups in the Ogaden recently told me:

After the war we came to the conclusion that enough was enough. Sure it would have been nice if we'd won but the fact was that we were beaten. We did our best, we put in everything we had, and they still beat us. So we decided, no more fighting. We looked around and saw that the government was keen to promote this idea of the equality of nationalities within Ethiopia and we made up our minds that we were going to go out and get our share. The Somalis are one of the nationalities of this country, with the same rights as everyone else. What we are doing is exercising those rights to get the things that we want.

It is my personal belief, from talks with many highly placed Ethiopian officials, that Eritrea and Tigre would *not* be oppressed if the EPLF and TPLF gave up armed struggle and came to the negotiating table. On the contrary I believe that the central government would go out of its way to accommodate the demands of the two groups. This is a government that has consistently dug its heels in and become stubborn when challenged or threatened but that has responded generously and imaginatively to those who have shown themselves willing to respect and listen to its points of view. I believe that such generosity and imagination would apply in Tigre and Eritrea if the challenges of the EPLF and the TPLF were withdrawn, and that the government would be willing to make many more far-reaching concessions than those that it has already indicated it will make in various policy statements, notably the Nine-Point Peace Plan for Eritrea. The Plan envisages the following:

(1) Full participation by Eritreans in the political, economic and social life of Ethiopia.

(2) Affirmation of the right of self-determination of nationalities through regional autonomy which takes due account of objective realities prevailing in Ethiopia; each of the regions of the country would be studied with the aim of determining at an appropriate time the format of the regions that can exist in the future.

(3) Urgent priority discussions with progressive groups and organizations in Eritrea to give immediate autonomy to Eritrea.

(4) Full government support to the progressive forces of Eritrea in their struggle to crush the three enemies of the broad masses of the Ethiopian people: feudalism, bureaucratic capitalism and imperialism.

(5) Immediate government assistance for the return of all Ethiopians who have fled to neighbouring and other countries because of lack of peace in Eritrea.

(6) A special government effort to rehabilitate those who have lost their properties, jobs and places in school because of dislocation caused by the Eritrean problem.

(7) Those imprisoned would be released; those sentenced to life imprisonment or death would have their cases reviewed as soon as peaceful conditions are restored.

(8) The state of emergency would be lifted as soon as peace is guaranteed in Eritrea.

(9) A special commission to be established to work out details of the programme.

Although the Nine-Point Plan was dismissed out of hand by all
the Eritrean liberation fronts when it was first published, it is
not a hollow document and represents a genuine effort by
Ethiopia's revolutionary regime to come to grips with the problems posed by the diverse ethnic, linguistic and religious groups
within the country.

The Somali experience in the aftermath of the Ogaden war is
one indication that the government is committed, in practice as
well as in rhetoric, to realizing the ideal of equal rights and equal
responsibilities for all Ethiopians.

Another pointer in this direction was the setting up in 1983
of the Institute for the Study of Ethiopian Nationalities. The
Institute, which initially reported directly to the Committee for
Organizing the Workers' Party of Ethiopia and now reports to
the Central Committee of the Party itself, is no mere academic
body but is in fact extremely powerful in influencing policy.
According to the government-owned *Ethiopian Herald*:

> Among the tasks of the Institute, are to identify and register
> all Ethiopian nationalities and record the population size of
> each, and to study the economic, cultural and social life and
> stage of development of each. The Institute will also carry
> out constitutional studies on the basis of which the People's
> Democratic Republic of Ethiopia is to be guided and adminis-
> tered.

Concealed within the verbiage, the indications are that the revolution is prepared to go to considerable lengths to foster 'unity
in diversity' and, given the opportunity, will seek to avoid
further head-on collisions of the kind it has experienced in Eritrea
and Tigre, preferring instead to neutralize potential conflicts by
making government as broadly based as possible. Whether it
will be feasible for it to follow this road, or whether it will be
goaded into taking a harsher and more extreme line, are questions
that have great bearing on the future peace and prosperity of the
country. They are questions to which answers must be sought
not only in Ethiopia but also in the trading and strategic policies
of the big and not-so-big powers and in the overall attitude that
the international community takes to Ethiopia's problems.

CHAPTER THREE

Guns and Butter

The Soviet Union, the United States, and the greater or lesser European powers are all keenly interested in what happens in Ethiopia and in the Horn of Africa as a whole. This interest, however, is not motivated by concern for the welfare of the people of the region. Neither is there any element of economic calculation in it, for Ethiopia, and its neighbours Sudan, Somalia and Djibouti, have virtually nothing to offer in the way of minerals or raw materials that the world does not already have in abundance elsewhere. In fact almost the sole importance of the Horn to the industrialized nations lies in the geographical accident of its location astride strategic shipping lanes close to the oil fields of the Arabian Gulf. Commanding the narrow Straits of Bab-el-Mandeb, Ethiopia—or a power allied to it—would be able to close the Red Sea in the event of global hostilities and would be well placed to control or disrupt the oil output of Arabia.

Ethiopia's strategic significance has, on the one hand, given the country some bargaining power which it otherwise might not have had—and bargaining power is a scarce and desirable commodity for any Third World government to possess. This plus, however, is outweighed by a long series of minuses, well summed up by historian Basil Davidson in a letter to *The Times* of London:

Much in the recent and present disasters of Ethiopia has derived, if indirectly, from external rivalries for influence in Addis Ababa, above all though by no means only between the superpowers. . . . If the region could be removed from the influence of external ambitions—or, at least, if the divisive force of such ambitions could be steadily reduced—the settlement of apparently intractable conflicts would be far less difficult than it is now.

What Basil Davidson is referring to is the tragic fact that, because of its strategic significance, the Horn has become a zone of superpower conflict by proxy. The Warsaw Pact on the one hand, and NATO and its allies on the other, have actively sought clients in the region and, by arming these clients and promoting their disputes, have turned this part of Africa into a dangerous and unstable powder keg. The Horn is more highly militarized in per capita terms than almost anywhere else in the Third World and this militarization has contributed directly to the region's poverty. Whatever agricultural or environmental measures are introduced, the development problems of the Horn of Africa— paramount amongst them susceptibility to famines—are not going to be solved until the local arms race ceases.

Ethiopia, which desperately needs to concentrate all its resources on development, currently spends some $440 million each year on its military forces. It has the largest army in black Africa—306,000 men in 1984—which includes one armoured division with 900 tanks, 23 infantry divisions, four parachute-commando brigades, 30 artillery batallions and 30 air defence battalions. The 2,500 strong navy, based at the Red Sea ports of Assab and Massawa, has two frigates, nine large patrol craft, seven fast attack craft, three coastal patrol craft, and one landing ship. The air force, with an establishment of 3,500, has 10 fighter ground-attack squadrons of which one has 10 MiG–17s, six have 100 MiG-21s and one has 12 Sukhois.

Somalia, which invaded Ethiopia during the Ogaden war in 1977, also has large and well-equipped armed forces on which it currently spends about $170 million a year. Its 60,000-strong army is supported by an irregular militia and para-military force of some 40,000. Its air force has 64 combat aircraft and its navy, with bases at Mogadishu, Kismayu and Berbera, has 10 fast attack craft, five large patrol craft and one tank landing craft.

The main beneficiaries of the militarization of the Horn of Africa are the Russians and the Americans.

From the mid 1960s through until 1977 the Soviet Union was closely identified with Somalia where in 1975, at the height of its influence, it had an estimated 6,000 'military advisers' as well as a substantial air and naval base at Berbera on the Gulf of Aden. During this same period, the United States was Ethiopia's friend, supplying $270 million worth of arms and training some 3,000 Ethiopians at American military academies. There was also a major US communications base, Kagnew, located near the city of Asmara, which, at its peak, had 3,000 expatriate personnel.

The US-Ethiopian and Soviet-Somali alliances began to look slightly odd after Ethiopia's revolution in 1974. Despite its professed Marxism, however, the *Dergue* was in no hurry to change its armourer and relations with Washington remained proper, if not warm.

Then came the Somali invasion of Ethiopia in 1977. This was tacitly—the Somalis claim, explicitly—encouraged by the Carter administration. When push came to shove, however, the Americans fought shy of the direct backing that they had hinted they would provide for the Somali cause. Their only initiative was to renege on the existing agreement to supply arms to Ethiopia and to refuse export licences for approximately $200 million worth of weapons already bought and paid for. The Ethiopians, furious at what they regarded as American treachery, turned immediately to Moscow for the military supplies they now urgently needed and, despite the Soviet alliance with Somalia, were soon receiving huge consignments of arms by airfreight. At the same time, in what has been described as 'one of the greatest pieces of political opportunism in post-war history', the Russians cut back on and then stopped their arms shipments to Somalia. The Somalis responded by expelling all their Soviet advisers, allowing only a skeleton diplomatic contingent of six persons to remain.

In its first few months the Ogaden war went in favour of the Somalis. By December 1977, however, as Russian arms shipments to Ethiopia began to take effect, and as 18,000 Cuban troops were drafted into the front lines on the Ethiopian side, the picture began to change dramatically. The Somali advance quickly became bogged down and, in March 1978, a large Somali force was surrounded and massacred at the town of Jigjiga—a victory achieved by the surprise tactic of using giant Mil-6 helicopters to airlift armour, artillery and men behind the Somali lines. Two days later a humiliated President Mohamed Siyad Barre had withdrawn all his troops from Ethiopian soil.

There is no doubt that the Soviet Union learned important

military lessons from its involvement in the Ogaden conflict and benefited from being able to try out new weapons and new strategies in combat. Its main gain, however, was Ethiopia itself which had accepted more than $2 billion worth of arms on credit, thus acquiring a debt that it could not hope to repay quickly. Since the war with Somalia, the continuing and worsening internal conflicts in Eritrea and Tigre have further deepened Ethiopia's dependence on Soviet military assistance and have increased the debt to a staggering $3 billion, with estimated annual interest payments of $200 million. While Russia from time to time presses for repayment of the principal as well, it is clear that it regards the loan as a good investment because it gives unprecedented influence with the Ethiopian government. As long as this influence does not wane, as long as the Soviet Union feels that its strategic interests in Ethiopia are not threatened, it is likely to be content for the arms account to remain substantially in deficit.

Russia is not alone in being keen to promote military dependence in the Horn of Africa. According to Edmond J. Keller, Associate Professor of Political Science at the University of California, the Carter administration 'set in motion an encirclement strategy' immediately after the Ogaden war 'designed to woo Ethiopia's neighbours with military aid, a practice expanded by President Ronald Reagan.' Under Reagan's direction, Keller continues:

> the United States has developed a Rapid Deployment Force capable of projecting America's military power into the Middle East and Persian Gulf, the 'Arc of Crisis'. Annual joint exercises involve United States troops along with the forces of the host countries in the region—Egypt, Sudan, Kenya, Somalia and Oman. No United States troops are stationed permanently in these countries, but massive amounts of funds have been given in the form of military aid or invested in modernized local military facilities.

In Somalia in particular, which now looks to the West to underwrite well over half of its national budget, United States policy has become increasingly aggressive during the 1980s. Despite the bad human rights record of President Siyad Barre's regime, American military support has shown a sharp upward trend.

Berbera, previously a Soviet base, has now been taken over by the US and is being redeveloped to supplement the Indian Ocean facilities at Diego Garcia. Somalia also receives military supplies from a number of European countries, notably Italy, while, at the same time, loans from Saudi Arabia and the Gulf States have facilitated the purchase of further European arms on the open market. Egypt is a close ally and is the main source of spare parts for the Somali army's still substantial stock of Soviet weaponry.

The net result is that Somalia has been able to make good its losses in the Ogaden war and continues to represent a real external threat to Ethiopia's security—as, of course, does Ethiopia to the security of Somalia. That this is so, that the mutual antagonism continues, can clearly be seen to be a consequence of superpower policy. Both the Western and Eastern Blocs have clear vested interests in perpetuating the instability of the Horn because it is this very instability which allows them to exert influence over the governments of the region and thus to compete effectively with one another for strategic advantage in the Red Sea and the Indian Ocean.

Because of the adverse development implications of the Horn's militarization, the British voluntary agency Oxfam makes the following strong statement as part of its new public awareness campaign 'Hungry for Change':

No one in Britain can remain unaware of the suffering of the seven million people in the worst affected areas of Ethiopia. Drought has much to do with the calamity, but there are other factors that are equally important AND WHICH INVOLVE US. One of the most serious factors is the armed conflict between the government of Ethiopia and neighbouring Somalia, and with secessionist groups in the provinces of Tigre and Eritrea. Yet the world's super-powers are doing little to encourage an end to these hostilities. Instead they are selling the weapons that are used in the fighting. How can the situation improve when the ongoing armed struggle causes destruction and divisions among people? OUR POLITICAL LEADERS MUST PRESS FOR THE UN TO TAKE A LEAD IN FINDING A WAY TO END THE HOSTILITIES. SELLING WEAPONS WHICH PROLONG THIS CONFLICT IS WRONG, AND THE COST OF THESE WEAPONS IS A TERRIBLE DRAIN ON THE COUNTRIES CONCERNED.

The costs are not simply the direct ones—the hundreds of millions of dollars in interest charges on arms purchases—though these alone are damaging enough. Far more harmful in the long term is the distortion of the local economy that the arms race causes, a distortion that leads inexorably away from food self-reliance and towards food dependence. Foreign exchange is required to pay for weapons. And Ethiopia, overwhelmingly an agricultural country, can only raise foreign exchange by encouraging farmers to grow cash crops, notably coffee, for export. If the need for foreign exchange to buy guns were removed then the government would be in a position to promote the growing of *food crops* much more vigorously than it does at present, and it is only by growing more food crops that Ethiopia can ever hope to be able to feed itself.

The economic distortion caused by overemphasis on cash crops was illustrated in a bitterly ironic way in November 1984, at the height of the famine, when to avoid bread shortages in Addis Ababa and other cities, Ethiopia was obliged to spend almost eight million dollars of its coffee revenues importing 52,000 tonnes of French wheat.

A few weeks earlier, but very much a part of the same terrible irony, the British press was raising its hands in horror to report that Ethiopian fresh fruits and vegetables were being sold in the UK. On 30 October 1984 *The Sun* reported:

> Furious MPs protested last night about the import of fresh vegetables at the same time as Britain prepared to airlift urgent supplies to the famine-hit country. Dozens of cases of beans and green peppers were on sale yesterday at a wholesale market near London's Heathrow Airport. And thousands of pounds worth of other Ethiopian food—beans, melons and sweetcorn —went on sale at shops in London. Tory MP Teddy Taylor said the sale of vegetables here was 'crazy'. He added: 'I find it unbelievable that Ethiopia should be exporting food when their children are starving.' Fellow Tory MP Terry Dicks, whose Greater London constituency includes Heathrow, fumed: 'I'm amazed.'

Mr Dicks should not have been amazed, and there was nothing unbelievable about Ethiopia's vegetable sales. As the British importer, Christopher Sims, said, summing up volumes of learned debate in one sentence: 'They need to export food to earn hard currency.' To this bit of pithy South London common sense, he might well have added: 'because they need hard currency to buy guns. . . .'

The precise costs and long-term consequences of burgeoning military expenditures for the economies of Third World countries like Ethiopia have never been accurately assessed; however all the research in this area suggests that they are truly immense, that they may be among the three or four key factors in rendering underdevelopment a persistent, inescapable condition. Perhaps it is in arms purchases that a very large part of the answer may be found to the layman's question 'why can't *they* (the countries of the Third World) catch up with *us* (the industrialized nations)'. As Professor John Kenneth Galbraith pointed out on 19 October 1984, at a ceremony in the General Assembly Hall of the United Nations commemorating World Food Day:

> There is one investment, which is shouldered in these days by many agricultural countries, that the industrial lands did not have to make in their agricultural stage. That is investment in complex military hardware. The United States, in a comparable stage of development, was blessed by virtually no military expenditures at all. We agree that the industrial countries should be persuaded not to sell such weaponry to the new countries. But I also urge a renewed determination among the new countries—the countries of the agricultural system—not to buy. Nothing is less consistent with the agricultural stage of development than a complex and costly military apparatus.

It is not only by promoting militarization that both West and East are doing a disfavour to the people of Ethiopia, and to the developing nations as a group. The iniquities of the arms trade reflect a broader trading system that consistently takes more than it gives. In common with other Third World countries Ethiopia has been steadily impoverished by falling prices for its exports and by fluctuating markets which make it impossible for it to plan effectively from year to year. Another vital factor has been the cost of borrowing money to finance development projects. Ethiopia's debt service ratio (the proportion of exports required to cover interest payments on loans) stood at 20 per cent in 1984, up from 14.6 per cent in 1978. Total external debt to the West currently stands at around one billion dollars and, according to the International Monetary Fund, will double by 1990.

In this context, it is particularly apt to observe that, while the West is delighted to lend money to Ethiopia on near-usurious commercial terms, Western governments are not at all willing to help in Ethiopia's development by providing long-term bilateral project aid. Emergency assistance—doling out a few shiploads of surplus grains in response to public pressure—is one thing; really getting involved, to the extent of funding the kind of projects that might help Ethiopians to feed themselves, is quite another. The reason for this is quite simple: Ethiopia has adopted a political system that is at variance with the dominant capitalist and free-enterprise ideology of the West. Western leaders do not hide their disapproval. Thus, for example, as the *Guardian* reported on 29 November 1984:

> Britain has no plans to offer long-term development aid to Ethiopia because of the political character of the regime, Mr Timothy Raison, the Overseas Development Minister, said yesterday. Mr Raison, who returned from a three-day visit to Ethiopia yesterday, said it was not easy to get involved with projects which the British government deemed to be ineffective. He gave as an example the lack of private enterprise in agriculture.

Mr Raison is as good as his word. Although there has been a recent and very welcome write-off of £2.5 million of debt, Britain's long-term project aid to Ethiopia remains small—in 1983 it was just £13,000.

Neither does Britain stand alone in its desire to deny significant long-term help to Ethiopia. The Soviet Union, Ethiopia's armourer, gives almost no development aid at all beyond a stingy modicum of technical assistance in the setting up of a few large and inefficient factories. Likewise, at the other end of the international political spectrum, the United States is not directly involved in a single Ethiopian development project, and even Italy, Ethiopia's largest bilateral Western donor, has yet to disburse funds promised in 1983. As a result, despite its unusually severe problems, Ethiopia receives less aid, on a per capita basis, than any other country in the Third World—a figure of $4.80 per head was being used by the United Nations in 1984 and this figure has since had to be revised substantially downwards as a result of new census data which shows the Ethiopian population to be nearer to 42 million than to the previous estimate of 32 million on which the UN calculations were based.

Western governments have a bad habit of distinguishing between emergency humanitarian aid—which they claim to be most willing to give to Ethiopia—and long-term aid (which they do not give). Yet what, logically, could be more 'humanitarian' than providing direct, massive and lasting assistance to Ethiopian development projects which could enable the country and its people to move towards self-reliance?

Beyond attacking this particular example of doublethink in our countries' aid policies, it is also important for us in the West to question the easy assumption that our governments *are* in fact willing to provide humanitarian assistance to Ethiopia. No one can dispute the generosity of the public in Europe, Australasia and the United States in 1984–85 once the scale of the Ethiopian disaster was made known; however, the generosity of Western governments and institutions was much less self-evident. To be sure, large sums of money, and large quantities of food, were made available for the emergency aid programme. As it turned out, however, this was often achieved by robbing Peter to pay Paul. Thus, for example, the EEC emergency package for Ethiopia was put together by diverting food aid from other needy countries—for example Bangladesh and Egypt—rather than by creating any new special budget. And Britain's Prime Minister Margaret Thatcher was reported to have been amongst those EEC leaders who were most opposed to voting any extra funds for food aid. 'It's a good idea,' she was reported to have said with a characteristic shrug, 'but what is it going to cost?'

In Britain itself this callous official attitude to the value of human life resulted in a similar decision to fund emergency supplies for Ethiopia by poaching the existing (and already very small) foreign aid budget. At least one British MP, Mr Robert Kilroy Silk, was horrified to hear this and outspoken enough to say so in Parliament: 'This is absolutely disgraceful,' he rightly complained on 30 October 1984. 'The government has been giving everybody the impression that it is making significant extra funds available, when it is not giving a penny extra. This money would otherwise have gone to some other poor country. It is the poor robbing the poor.'

What was even more disgraceful was the fact that the British and other Western governments took no kind of initiatives themselves, but rather had to be *forced* to give emergency aid to Ethiopia by the tremendous public pressure that followed television coverage of the famine. One illustration of this is that Oxfam had been trying throughout 1984 to cajole the British government into action but was consistently snubbed until the story became world news. In an interview conducted as part of the research for this book, field officer Marcus Thompson observed:

> We would not have had the response of Western governments to the food emergency in Ethiopia without the anger expressed by the population. . . . When I telexed back from Ethiopia in August 1984 to say 'we should consider the purchase of around 10,000 to 20,000 tons of food', my colleagues here at Oxfam went immediately to the EEC and to the food aid arm of the British government and were told 'Sorry, there is nothing available, we have used up the allocations for this year'. So we went out and bought the grain ourselves. Since then both the EEC and the British government have gone back on their decisions. This wasn't because we asked. They didn't say to us 'Ah, we haven't got anything left, but we will reconsider'; they quite simply said to us 'We haven't got anything left'. No, it was when there was a major public and political outcry that they said 'Ah, we will reconsider'. Had it not been for that political outcry, I suggest they would not have reconsidered.

Marcus Thompson is right. Without the angry insistence of a concerned and caring public it is certain that the governments of the West would have been content to ignore the plight of Ethiopia entirely. It is, unfortunately, equally certain, after the public outcry dies down, that the problems of Ethiopia will once again be shelved by our bigoted and self-serving politicians.

At least, that is, until television carries into our living rooms the images of the next Ethiopian famine. . . .

PART TWO

Famine in Ethiopia

CHAPTER FOUR

The Curse of Famine

Ethiopia, unlike much of the rest of Africa, has a long recorded history. In the chronicles of bygone years, in the accounts of travellers who have visited the country, we can find haunting premonitions of the present tragedy. Images of death and destitution echo through the centuries, as though famine were a curse called down upon the Ethiopians at the beginning of time and never since lifted.

Over a thousand years ago the Christian Emperor of Ethiopia wrote the following in a letter to the Patriarch of Alexandria: 'Great tribulation hath come upon our land and all our men are dying of the plague, and our beasts and cattle have perished and God hath restrained the heavens so that they cannot rain. . . .'

Similar devastation occurred in the 12th century when, according to the chronicles: 'famine and plague broke out in the land, and the rain would not fall upon the fields. . . .'

A 13th-century manuscript records four major famines: 1252; 1258–59; 1261–62 and 1274–75, the latter being so severe that, as well as the peasantry, many noble families perished.

In the 14th century, according to another ancient text, a 'cruel famine' laid waste to the land during the reign of Emperor Amda Tseyon (1314–44).

One hundred years later Maqrizi, an Arab historian, tells us of a pestilence that ranged far and wide in the years 1435–36 and 'destroyed the inhabitants of Abyssinia'. Maqrizi's account is substantiated by the royal chronicle of Emperor Zara Yaqob (1434–68) which describes 'a great plague' that killed 'so large a number of persons that no one remained to bury the dead'. Another manuscript from the same century tells us that there 'arose against all men a murderous plague so great that it is impossible to describe'. Many people died and their houses were filled with 'tears and lamentations'.

The historical record improves in quality from the 16th century, recording no less than 23 major famines between 1540 and 1800, in the following years: 1540, 1543, 1567, 1611, 1623, 1625, 1633, 1634, 1635, 1636, 1650, 1653, 1678, 1700, 1702, 1747, 1748, 1752, 1783, 1789, 1796, 1797, and 1800.

The famine of 1540 is described by the chronicler of Emperor Galawdewos as an event of awesome proportions, 'the like of which had not been seen at the time of the kings of Samaria, nor at the time of the destruction of the Second Temple'. God, the writer continues, had in his fury: 'lit a fire which burnt to the very depths, devouring the soil and its fruits, and he sent on the earth the teeth of animals and the venom of serpents.' Food was so scarce that people were forced to grub for the roots of trees.

Some years later, drought struck again: 'Hunger and thirst became general, because there was neither food nor drink; illness reigned everywhere because there were no more cures; and all the people were seized by dejection because courage had disappeared.'

The 17th century seems to have been a particularly bad one for famines. The following account, written in 1625 by the Jesuit Jerome Lobo, is typical of many others:

Our house was perpetually surrounded by those unhappy people [victims of the famine], whom want had compelled to abandon their habitations and whose pale cheeks and meagre bodies were undeniable proofs of their misery and distress. All the relief I could possibly afford them could not prevent the deaths of such numbers that their bodies filled the highways; and to increase our affliction, the hyenas, having devoured the carcases, and finding no other food, fell upon the living; their natural fierceness being so increased by hunger that they dragged the children out of the very houses. I myself saw a troop of hyenas tear a child of six years old in pieces before I, or anyone else, could come to its assistance.

The first years of the reign of Emperor Fasilidas (1632–67) were marked by almost continuous devastation. A plague of locusts destroyed the crops, bringing in its wake famine and a widespread cholera epidemic that was named in Amharic *fangel* (the liquidator). 'Famine struck and after famine the plague,' recounts the chronicler, 'many died; others were stricken by terror and this was no help to them.'

During the repeated famines of the 18th century, 'all the provinces' were reported to have suffered 'great distress' and it became common for people to sell themselves or their children into bondage to the Emperor in order to escape death by starvation.

The first year of the 19th century, too, was itself a year of famine. Subsequently, crop failures, droughts, hunger and epidemics inflicted themselves upon Ethiopia with dismal regularity. Of the 1828–29 famine the visiting British surgeon, Charles Johnston, recalls in his memoirs: 'The people were reduced to the greatest extremity for food and clothing. Numbers fell victim from hunger alone and, to relieve their necessities, numerous acts of violence and robbery disturbed the usually peaceful state of society.'

The worst famine of all, however, occurred towards the end of the century in the years 1888–92. Still referred to as 'The Great Famine', this had a profound impact on Ethiopian society.

The problem began with a major outbreak of rinderpest, which, with the exception of a few isolated highland herds, completely destroyed the country's cattle stocks and drove into penury hundreds of thousands of Ethiopians who depended on cattle for their livelihoods. The rinderpest epidemic started in the north, as the result of the introduction of infected Indian cattle by the Italians who were at that time annexing Eritrea, and quickly spread south through Tigre, Wollo and Gonder into Shoa. By 20 February 1889, just four months after the first outbreak of rinderpest at Massawa, Count Antonelli, an Italian envoy, reported from Shoa that 'all Ethiopia' was threatened and that the epidemic could be 'fatal to her economic life'.

The loss of cattle had a direct effect on agriculture in that, without draught oxen, the peasants were unable adequately to plough and prepare their land. Added to this, the rains failed in 1889 and 1890 and the effects of the resulting drought were compounded by an unusual abundance of crop pests: locusts, caterpillars and rats. Inevitably the market prices for grain, particularly *teff* (used to make the Ethiopian staple *injera*), soared and soon only the very rich were able to buy bread. Starvation on a mass scale followed, producing conditions in many ways indistinguishable from those that prevail in Ethiopia today.

Looking at the accounts of the period left for us by contemporary observers it is difficult to avoid a strange reverse sense of *déjà vu*. A certain Father Picard, for example, describes large, straggling crowds of people wandering the highways, begging for succour in the name of the Holy Virgin. Such crowds throng the roads not far north of Addis Ababa today. Another missionary, M. Coulbeaux, wrote on 30 March 1890: 'Everywhere I meet walking skeletons and even horrible corpses, half eaten by hyenas, of starvelings who had collapsed from exhaustion.' Those skeletons still walk today, their bones trembling in the bleak winter winds of Korem and Makalle. An Ethiopian Protestant minister, Mikael Argawi, reported of conditions in Tigre in 1890: 'Thousands are dying. The famine is indescribable. The well-to-do and the poor are alike carried away by hunger and pestilence. Such a famine has never befallen our land.' Of the 1984 famine, too, people are saying: 'Such a one we have never seen before. . . .'

It is probable that as much as two-thirds of the entire population of Ethiopia died during the Great Famine of 1888–92. The same catastrophe would certainly have been repeated during the current famine had it not been for the last-minute emergency relief programme that began to get underway in October 1984. Too little and too late as it was, international aid did at least mitigate the effects of the drought to a small degree so that the people of Ethiopia were spared the worst privations suffered by their great-grandparents a century before.

Lest we forget, it is worth recounting some of those extreme privations as they were witnessed by observers at the time and which, taken together, constitute a travelogue of hell. It is the same hell into which the victims of the 1984–85 famine were plunged, but even deeper and more terrible caverns were visited.

The words of the Italian diplomat, Martini (a future Governor of Eritrea), bear quotation at length because they reveal the kind of horrors that would undoubtedly have occurred by the end of 1984 at Korem, at Makalle, at Bati and throughout northern Ethiopia—indeed which so very nearly *did* occur—had not international aid at last begun to arrive. Describing the scene at Massawa in 1891, Martini reported:

Here and there were abandoned corpses, their faces covered with rags; one, horrible to see, appeared to move, so swarming was it with insects that crept over the decomposing limbs in the burning sun. The dead awaited the hyenas, the living awaited death. From a thicket issued a thin murmur of voices, while hands devoid of flesh stretched forward quaking with the last shiver of life. Here, in the sand, a dying man with his last energy raises himself on his back, glares with staring, glassy and unseeing eyes, gives out a rattle and drops to the ground, striking his neck and his back as he falls. There a crouching woman who can no longer speak rocks with continuous motion a child of four or five years near to exhaustion and, devoting herself to her pallid dear one, mutters *miskin, miskin* ('shame, shame') in a faint, hoarse voice. We are accosted for help, and, from their death beds, suddenly rise a mob of skeletons whose bones can be seen under the taut skin as in the mummified skeleton of Saint Bernard. They try to follow us, they also crying out *miskin, miskin*; exhausted, they fall down, attempt to rise, stumble, fall again, and trail behind us on all fours, calling for help with groans and shrieks. Mothers exhaustedly heave their sucklings from the ground and follow us weeping and moaning, and pointing for us at their shrivelled breasts. We distribute some *lire*, a form of succour laughable in such indigence, useless to those who will be dead in an hour. . . . I flee to escape from it and stumble on young boys searching in the excrement of camels to find a grain of *dura*; horrified, I turn away only to see other boys whom the local police are driving away by force from the carcase of a horse, the stinking left-over of the hyenas. From this carcase they snatch—biting with their teeth at its entrails —the entrails because they are softer, softer because they are more putrid. I flee, horrified, stupefied, shamed by my impotence, hiding my watch chain in shame, ashamed in myself of the breakfast which I had eaten, of the dinner which awaited me. . . .

Martini's description is particularly vivid. But that he was not exaggerating the horrendous consequences of extreme hunger is borne out in many other accounts. Afewerk Gebre Yesus, an Ethiopian observer of the Great Famine, wrote:

The people were dying of starvation along the routes, in the fields, in churchyards, and in the compounds of the nobility.

The time was a time of festivity for hyenas and vultures and of misery for human beings. Let alone people expressing sympathies for each other, a mother no longer wept for her child nor a child for his mother. Burial of the dead became rare; at that time to be buried was reserved for the fortunate ones. The rest were 'buried' in the stomachs of hyenas and vultures.

Worse was to come. As the famine reached its peak, outbreaks of cannibalism—a practice utterly foreign to Ethiopian culture —became commonplace. One such incident is described by Gebre Yesus, the case of a woman suspected of killing and eating a number of children, who was arrested and brought before Emperor Menelik II.

The Emperor asked her whether it was true that she ate human flesh. She said: 'Yes, Your Majesty, I ate seven children when I was extremely hungry'. The Emperor again asked: 'Where did you catch them and how did you kill them?' She replied: 'I strangled them when they were playing'. But the woman did not look like a person who had eaten anything, let alone seven children. Her bare belly looked like the dewlap of a starved cow. Her eyes were swollen and she looked pale. She gave the impression of a person about to fall. Menelik said: 'What can one do? It is the times'. He ordered clothes and food for her and handed her over to an officer.

Eight years after the end of the Great Famine, the 20th century dawned on an Ethiopia still beset by medieval problems. People had been dying of hunger for a thousand years and it seemed perfectly acceptable and reasonable that they should go on doing so for another thousand. There was, accordingly, little surprise when a widespread famine struck the country in 1916 and lasted until 1920. No one was amazed when, in 1927–28, drought and mass starvation hit the provinces of Wollo, Tigre, and Gonder, as well as the northern parts of Shoa. Famine recurred in 1934–35 and again in 1947–50—this time predominantly in lowland regions. By 1957–58 the highlands of Tigre were starving once again, and in 1964–65 it was the turn of Wollo. In this latter famine some 40,000 people starved to death in the district of Lasta, partly because of the neglect of the governor who failed to collect relief grain that had been made available in the regional capital Dessie.

Despite Emperor Haile Selassie's reputation as a modernizer, the record from the 1940s onwards shows that in one area at least —Ethiopia's gross susceptibility to famines—he was content to preserve the *status quo*. Tourist roads may have been built, airports inaugurated and a national airline launched, but at no point was any government body established to address itself directly to meeting the challenge of hunger. The bureaucracy was unmotivated and indifferent, preferring to let people die rather than to take action on their behalf.

This official neglect, evident on a small scale in the correspondingly small Wollo famine of 1964–65, was thrown into stark relief by the giant proportions of the next famine, also centred in Wollo, which began in 1971 and which, by 1974, was to lead to the overthrow of the Emperor.

The first reports of crop failure in Wollo were made in October 1971 by the chief municipal officer of the town of Alamata, who suggested that some kind of relief operation was certainly going to be needed otherwise the people of the province would starve. In November, the regional governor wrote to the provincial governor asking him to specify the amount and kind of relief that would be appropriate to solve the problem. The provincial governor, a good bureaucrat, responded 38 days later with a memo asking for specific guidance as to how he should compile, order and present the required information. In the absence of a reply he did the safe thing and set up a committee to 'study' the matter. This committee studied for three months and passed on its report to the Ministry of the Interior in April 1972. A month later, in May 1972, the Ministry of the Interior decided that the problem did not properly fall within its domain and referred the report to the Ministry of Community Development and Social Affairs. Finally, in June 1972, more than eight months after the crop failures in Wollo had first been observed, the Grain Deficit Study Committee of the Ministry of Community Development convened to discuss the problem.

The Grain Deficit Study Committee, swollen with the pomp of its own high title, rejected out of hand the report that had been put before it, claiming that both the extent of the drought, and the numbers of people said to be affected, were exaggerations. The Committee instructed the Ministry of the Interior to prepare a new report and, more than a month later, at the end of July 1972, the Ministry of the Interior passed back this instruction to the regional office in Dessie. The regional office, in turn, instructed the provincial office in Alamata to prepare a new report. However, by August 1972, no new report had been submitted.

In September, when the situation in Wollo was already out of control with looting and starvation widespread, the provincial office finally submitted its report. The regional office, now inundated with similar reports from other provinces, referred the matter relatively quickly to the Ministry of Community Development and, in October 1972, a recommendation was made to the Council of Ministers that 2,000 tonnes of relief grain should be sent to Wollo (as against the original figure of 68,000 tonnes to cover estimated needs). In November 1972 the regional office was told to collect its derisory 2,000 tonnes from Asmara —several days' journey away by road. Unfortunately, however, no government transport was available to move the consignment and funds had to be raised privately in Dessie to hire trucks. It was not until January 1973, therefore—one year, two months and seven days after the problem had first been identified—that the first relief grain was actually delivered in Wollo.

The poor by this time had begun to vote with their feet and, during the first months of 1973, columns of destitute people could be seen marching on Addis Ababa from all directions—a true crusade of hunger. The almost criminal stupidity of the bureaucracy, which had done nothing while the famine grew to such proportions, was now compounded by the fiendish efficiency of the army which was sent out to round up the starving and return them to their homes to die. While this was going on, the Ministry of Information launched a campaign intended to convince both the Ethiopian public and the international community that there was no famine nor any problem of hunger other than limited, localized food shortages.

In the face of the horrifying reality of what was happening in Wollo, of mass starvation, and of a death toll in excess of 200,000,* the official conspiracy of silence did not prove effective for long. As we have seen, it was finally broken wide open by a foreigner—television producer Jonathan Dimbleby, who visited the country in September 1973, went to Wollo, and

* Encyclopaedia Britannica (1979) - at least 50,000, perhaps as many as 100,000 died

filmed the terrible things he saw there. Ethiopia's secret famine was a secret no longer.

The reaction of Ethiopians to the irrefutable revelation of their own government's callous irresponsibility was deep anger. This anger, in turn, woke them up from the slumber of ages and, within a year, the Imperial order had been overthrown. It was as though in learning about the famine the people of Ethiopia had also, for the first time, learned the true nature of the regime under which they lived—and had understood that they could change it.

The Imperial indifference to the 1972–74 tragedy, which cost Haile Selassie his throne, demonstrates a lasting truth: bad government, every bit as much as bad weather, has been the crucial factor in the historical susceptibility of the Ethiopian peasantry to drought and famine. Summing up this truth in the 18th century the Scottish traveller James Bruce, who visited Ethiopia during one of its periodic famines, wrote: 'Large ants, and prodigious swarms of rats and mice . . . consume immense quantities of grain. To these plagues may be added still one, the greatest of them all, bad government, which speedily destroys all the advantages they [the Ethiopian people] reap from nature, climate, and situation.'

Throughout the recorded history of famine in Ethiopia—from the ninth century until the overthrow of Haile Selassie—there is no record of any consistent or well thought-out programme to meet the challenge of hunger. Better governments made piecemeal attempts to feed the poor in lean years, worse governments turned their backs and let the starving peasants die like flies—but both the better and the worse seem to have agreed that there was really very little to be done.

Fittingly, since the revolution that took place in Ethiopia in 1974 was born out of a reaction against this kind of official neglect, the current government *does* have a policy aimed at ending hunger once and for all, and has created a formidable mechanism to implement this policy. Through the Relief and Rehabilitation Commission, a sustained and committed effort has been made, at least in this crucial area, to be a 'good government' in the way that past regimes were not. Though not necessarily an indication that this effort has failed, the famine of 1984–85 has signalled how very much still remains to be done.

CHAPTER FIVE

The Build-up to 1984

The existence of famine in Ethiopia shocked and surprised millions of people around the world when it hit the headlines in the last quarter of 1984. The story was old hat to aid workers in the country itself, however, and to the staff of Ethiopia's Relief and Rehabilitation Commission, who had been issuing warnings of the impending disaster for three years.

As early as May 1981, in a presentation to the United Nations Conference on Least Developed Countries, the RRC described an alarming deterioration in weather conditions in Ethiopia with rain failures and drought becoming the norm in many parts of the country. This, it was predicted, would certainly lead to famine unless swift action involving the international community were taken. 'To alleviate the suffering of the people,' the RRC admonished, 'emergency assistance, such as grain, supplementary food, edible oil, drugs, vaccines, transportation and communication facilities, are urgently required.'

The warnings continued, growing in stridency and frequency, throughout 1982 and 1983; however, they aroused absolutely no international interest.

By the beginning of 1984 Ethiopia faced an emergency on a quite unprecedented scale and, in March of that year, the RRC reported that upwards of five million people were now affected by famine. This report was picked up by the Western media, received some response from the Western public, but, other than eliciting a few lethargic pledges, was ignored by Western governments (and, needless to say, by Eastern Bloc governments as well which, if anything, have consistently proved themselves to be even more indifferent to the fate of the hungry in Ethiopia than their counterparts in the West).

In August 1984 the RRC made this disturbing statement at an international gathering in Addis Ababa:

We have had no grain in our stocks since mid-July. The situation becomes even more grave when one sees the uncertainties of the March pledges by donors. Since our March appeal roughly 87,000 tonnes of grain and 8,000 tonnes of supplementary food were expected. Unfortunately, however, no shipment of the pledged food has yet been received. Despite our repeated requests to donors to push forward the arrival time of food commodities, the response is still very slow. . . .

After providing a detailed outline, province by province, of the state of 'creeping drought' that had overtaken the country, the Commission concluded that the total number of people affected was now around six million and that the *minimum* requirement for food aid for the next five months was therefore 400,000 tonnes: 'The gathering famine is approaching its height and every minute of delay means further aggravation of the problem.'

It was not until late October 1984, when the BBC film exposed the true extent and horror of the Ethiopian disaster, and when people of the industrialized nations began to demand action from their governments, that the brakes were taken off and that food aid began to be despatched in significant quantities.

That it had taken so long for this to happen was nothing short of scandalous. As Relief and Rehabilitation Commissioner Dawit Wolde-Ghiorgis commented at the time:

The pledges made after March were nowhere near our requirements, and quite a few of these pledges started arriving in Ethiopia only five months after our appeal. . . . We would never be able to have an accurate estimate of the lives lost and the number of malnourished persons and displaced people caused by the irresponsible and indifferent attitude of certain governments and organizations who had the capacity to do better. It was not lack of sympathy or understanding amongst the public. It was not lack of information. Neither was it lack of food or funds because we realize that in Europe and North America the public is swimming in abundance. It could never be anything else except sheer apathy, or politicization of humanitarian aid. . . .

Later, in December 1984, Dawit elaborated on this theme when, while thanking donors for their efforts since October, he observed:

> What makes us angry, and deeply sad at the same time, is that what is happening in many parts of the country now could so easily have been prevented. From the beginning of the year we predicted that, unless there was a massive inflow of grain, funds and other relief supplies, the situation would deteriorate appallingly. . . . I cannot overemphasize the growing sense of shock that my staff and I felt when we realized that first our March appeal and then our August appeal had failed, when the days of indifference turned into the months of apathy, especially when we could see that—all around the country— our predictions were turning horribly true. An almost inconceivable nightmare was happening: Ethiopia was being forgotten by a world glutted with a surplus of grain; its humanitarian advocates had disappeared.

The 1984 famine, the latest in the long line of Ethiopian disasters that stretches back through recorded history, had deep and widely-spread roots.

Many factors were at work in ensuring that it was exceptionally severe. Of these, the indifferent and slow international response was amongst the most important—since, had it been quicker, tens of thousands of lives could certainly have been saved. It is wrong of Ethiopia, however, to blame its troubles entirely on the international community. The current state of political and economic disruption within the country, particularly in Eritrea, Tigre and Wollo, also played a major role in ensuring that the famine was worse than it otherwise might have been, and this, ultimately, is a problem that the Ethiopians themselves are going to have to solve; no one else can be expected to put their house in order.

Neither should the role of natural factors be forgotten. In the final analysis, it was drought that triggered the 1984 famine. Drought on its own, however, is not necessarily a killer; it became a killer in this case because it occurred in a desperately poor and underdeveloped country that had few friends in the international community and that was, at the same time, acutely destabilized internally by secessionist wars. In addition, it occurred in a country where environmental degradation, in the form of erosion and deforestation, has been going on for centuries.

According to United Nations estimates, Ethiopia currently loses around 1.6 billion tonnes of its precious topsoil every year through wind and water erosion. This process is particularly advanced in the highlands where pressure of population has meant that fields which should have been left fallow have been repeatedly ploughed and reused, a tradition that, over a period of many years, has sucked out essential nutrients and turned good soil into infertile dust.

Another harmful practice in the north has been the farming of marginal lands, for example on exposed slopes. Here, once the protective vegetation cover has been removed, the thin topsoils have simply been washed away.

Deforestation, again largely a consequence of excessive population pressure, has also been a major factor—since trees play a vital role in retaining friable soils. A century ago about 44 per cent of Ethiopia was forested; however the incessant search for fuelwood and construction timber by the ever-burgeoning population meant that, by 1950, the forest area had been reduced to 16 per cent. Today it is down to just 4 per cent—all of which is in the south; the north is completely bald.

A final cause of erosion has been, at least until very recently, consistently poor and unplanned management of water resources. This meant, according to Oxfam, that

water cascaded off the bare slopes at high speed, washing topsoil indiscriminately off the land during the rainy season; while in the drought there was no reservoir from which to irrigate crops. The rain also washed loose stones and boulders, once anchored by tree roots, from the hilltops down into the fields below, making the land more difficult to work and further decreasing its fertility. What protective vegetation remained after every available hectare had been cultivated was grazed and trampled to extinction.

In every sense, therefore, looked at from all possible angles, Ethiopia is a country that is ripe for ecological disaster. Prior to the 1972–74 famine, and to the revolution, nothing was done to reduce its vulnerability. And, in the post-revolutionary decade, although important steps have been taken, there has simply not been time to achieve very much—there has been no let-up, no period of plenty in which Ethiopians could put new plans into action to see them through the lean years. On the contrary, the 1984 famine is better regarded as an extension and a continuation of that of 1972–74 than as a separate phenomenon.

Thus, even while Wollo and Tigre were desperately attempting to recover from the effects of the 1972–74 famine, the south-eastern lowlands of Harerghe and Bale were falling into the grip of an equally severe drought which by 1975 had seriously —and probably permanently—disrupted the way of life of the nomadic pastoralists of the Ogaden. This disruption was further complicated by the Ogaden war of 1977–78 which so drained national resources that development programmes in all other provinces were also affected.

Severe drought in the south-east continued throughout 1979 and only began to ease in 1980—the year in which, with cruel irony, renewed signs of deterioration in the northern provinces began to be noticed. According to an Oxfam study:

> In 1980 the rains on the eastern escarpment and lowlands of Tigre were 30 per cent of normal, reducing crop yields and culling livestock. The 1981 rains were worse still for many parts of the province. . . . In Tigre and Eritrea, the failure of the 1982 rains meant that, for five or six seasons in succession, the harvest had been poor. Eritrean *dura* (sorghum) prices more than doubled in 1982, but people in drought areas managed to survive by eating wild fruits such as cactus and wild grass seeds. The central highlands and eastern lowlands of Tigre were particularly hard hit in 1981 and, with the failure of the 1982 rains, this area broadened into a belt stretching from Adwa to Enderta districts. There was scarcely any harvest in some areas of northern Wollo, eastern Gonder, and central and north-eastern Tigre in 1982.

In the provinces of Gonder, Wollo, Tigre and Eritrea, some 2,270,000 people were affected by the drought conditions of 1982—up from 1,850,000 the year before. By July 1983, however, with yet another almost complete failure of the rains, the affected population of these four provinces had risen to 3,400,000. Elsewhere in Ethiopia, regions which had never before experienced severe droughts—northern Sidamo, parts of

Shoa, and the province of Gamo Goffa—were beginning to suffer the same kind of devastation that had been visited upon the north and it was clear that a truly epic national disaster was in the making.

Ethiopian agriculture revolves around the country's two principal rainy seasons: *belg* (February to May) and *meher* (June to September). Lowlanders traditionally plant long-maturing crops such as maize and sorghum during the *belg* season. Highlanders, in the different climate of the mountains, take advantage of the *belg* rains to plant short-maturing crops such as barley and wheat which they then harvest in June and July. The *meher* rains allow the planting of long-maturing grains in highland areas and the resulting crop is normally harvested in November/December.

In the second half of 1983 the *meher* rains, on which Ethiopians had been counting to reverse the losses of the previous bad seasons, proved disappointing. According to the National Meteorological Services Agency, precipitation was down to about half of normal right across the country with no rain at all in many areas. At the same time, a greatly increased rate of surface water evaporation was noted, coupled with a reduction in underground water levels. Hitherto perennial wells and rivers dried up, and pastoralists in the lowland areas were forced to drive their herds out of the traditional grazing grounds in search of water, causing profound ecological imbalances. More than one million head of cattle perished in Sidamo province alone. Meanwhile, in the highlands, the poor rains led to a drastically reduced harvest in November 1983 and, throughout vast areas of the north, hunger became commonplace.

The next blow fell in February/March 1984 when it became clear that the *belg* rains had failed entirely. The highland farmers' fast-maturing crops died in the ground while, in most areas, the long-maturing crops of the lowlanders were not even planted. By now more than five million people were estimated to be affected by the drought.

The *coup de grace* was delivered by the sporadic performance of the *meher* rains which started late, fell lightly, if at all, and, in all parts of the country, were over by the end of August 1984, a month earlier than normal. According to a report prepared by the Food and Agriculture Organization of the United Nations this meant that Ethiopia's total crop production for 1984 would be severely curtailed: down by at least 30 per cent on the year before with a resultant shortfall of between 1.7 and 2 million tonnes. 'This,' said the FAO, 'may be roughly equivalent to the ordinary consumption of between 6.5 and 8 million persons.'

By October 1984 hunger in Ethiopia had become starvation, and the FAO's dry statistics were being borne out in millions of individual tragedies. The columns of famished and emaciated people trekking from the barren, eroded farmlands of the north into relief camps that did not have food in sufficient quantities to meet even a fraction of their needs posed a problem for which there was no easy solution. It was already clear, as a result of the bad *meher* rains, that the November harvest was going to be pitifully small. This meant, unless international food aid could be mobilized virtually overnight and on a massive scale, that those who were starving now would soon begin to die.

CHAPTER SIX

A Journey in Hell

This is what happens to you when you starve.

As your intake of food falls below the normal level, you at first experience severe and racking hunger pangs. These do not last, however. The body adapts within a matter of days, and the pain goes.

To meet your energy needs—for example, the energy required to walk in search of food, or to beg on a street corner—you are now living off your own stores of fat. Depending on just how fat you were when the famine started, these reserves may last you for a week, or two, or three; but sooner or later they will be gone.

Your body then has no option but to start metabolizing tissue protein—in other words, your muscles—and as this happens you begin to feel listless and depressed, too tired to work. Your intellect will probably still be clear at this stage; but your personality will already have undergone some marked changes. Fairly early on, for example, you lose interest in sex; reproduction, your body tells you, is no longer a priority. A little later you become irritable, subject to irrational and impotent rages. In the last stages of hunger you find it difficult to concentrate, and become introspective and increasingly indifferent to your own fate—in short, you no longer give a damn whether you live or die.

This is probably just as well, because the physiological degradation that you go through during starvation is unpleasant. Most notable is the loss of body weight—which can drop to about half of normal. Emaciation is particularly obvious around your thighs, buttocks and ribs where protruding bones give you the appearance of a skeleton some time before you expire. Your hair turns dull and starts to drop out. At the same time your skin pales, takes on a piebald, patchy pigmentation and becomes dry, loose and brittle. You suffer from hypothermia—abnormally low body temperature—and, as you lose your ability to shiver, you become susceptible to the slightest change in the weather; a cold night can be terminal. Sapped of your vital energies, you also fall easy prey to all manner of relatively minor infections: bronchitis and pneumonia, flu and diarrhoea all become killers.

Bad for adults, starvation is truly terrible in its consequences for infants. A famine, like that currently raging in Ethiopia, can have effects that rebound down the generations, since not only will it kill tens of thousands of children, but it will also impair for life many of those who survive.

The damage to the children begins even before they are born. Poorly nourished mothers give birth to weak, underweight babies who, in many cases, will quickly die: some 30 to 40 per cent of all infant deaths in developing countries are attributable to low birth weight, and this percentage rises steeply during famine conditions.

Those babies who do not die at birth still face a daunting steeplechase of diseases related to malnutrition.

The best known and most prevalent of these conditions is marasmus, characterized in infants by marked growth failure and bodies shrunken to below 60 per cent of normal weight. The face of a child suffering from marasmus appears strangely aged and shrivelled like that of a monkey, or a head-hunter's grisly trophy. His body is wasted, with match-stick limbs draped in flaccid, leathery skin. Too weak to move, or to cry, he lies dully in a pool of his own diarrhoea.

With his natural immunity and resistance to disease gone, the child with marasmus suffers from—and eventually may be killed by—acute gastroenteritis. He is not alone: in the developing world as a whole five million infants every year, about one child every six seconds, die from diarrhoea. Other killer diseases commonly linked to marasmus include pneumonia and tuberculosis.

Marasmus—the word is derived from the Greek *marainein*, meaning 'to waste'—is really nothing more than a fancy name for starvation in children. There is another condition, sometimes associated with famines, which is produced not so much by complete absence of food as by a diet that does not contain enough *good* food. This disease is called kwashiorkor (which in the Ga language of Ghana means: 'the disease the first child gets when the next one is on the way').

A child suffering from kwashiorkor does not at first sight appear hungry, because he has a rather jolly pot belly. He *is* hungry, however—for protein, of which he is in urgent need. A closer look reveals how bad his condition is: terrible lesions and open sores are common, and the skin is frequently flaky and cracked. His hair loses its original colour, usually turning red in African children. His liver is enlarged and fatty and he suffers from severe anaemia.

A third disease prevalent amongst children in famine areas is xerophthalmia, blindness that is caused by malnutrition-related vitamin-A deficiency. Worldwide, this terrible condition is estimated to blind some 500,000 children each year—despite the fact that it is extremely inexpensive to treat. For the price of one main-battle tank it would be possible to do wonders.

Inevitably, xerophthalmia is common in the relief camps in Ethiopia. The majority of the children already show the early symptoms of the disease—notably the characteristically 'muddy' appearance of the normally white conjunctiva. In others, blindness is more advanced, with the original brown colouring of the iris overlaid by a milky-blue film. In others still the whole structure of the cornea has visibly softened in an irreversible process known medically as colliquative necrosis. The final stage of the disease is particularly hideous to observe. The eye comes to resemble a poached egg. The lens swells and falls out leaving only a rotten, gaping socket.

Blind, wasted children, children racked with diarrhoea, children wheezing out their lives in the last agonizing stages of pneumonia, children who would never know the joy of laughter, children too weak even to seek the release of tears, children parted from their dead mothers, hopeless, hungry, abandoned children—it was these tragic images of the lost young of Ethiopia that I carried home with me, foremost in my thoughts, after visiting the famine-devastated provinces of Wollo and Tigre in November and December 1984. Later, so that I could continue to function normally, I found that I had to bury my recollections, inter them in remote regions of my mind where they would not interfere with the day-to-day running of my life. Now as I write, I feel that I am standing beside an open grave. . . .

When I arrived in Addis Ababa and started on the wearying

bureaucratic paper-chase that is always involved in getting a provincial travel permit, one of the first things that struck me was how busy the sleepy Ethiopian capital had become. Things were booming. In an odd, ironic way, the famine was obviously good for business. The Hilton hotel, which normally struggles to reach 50 per cent room occupancy, was full to bursting point: would-be guests were being turned away in droves, and rumour had it that a number of United Nations aid experts had elected to sleep in the sauna rather than brave the rigours of one of the down-town hotels.

As an ex-journalist myself, I could not help noticing also that the city was full of hacks. The 70-strong East Africa press corps from Nairobi seemed to have migrated here *en masse* and, in addition, most of the leading American, British and European dailies had sent out correspondents.

As is usual when large numbers of scribes are gathered together on a 'story', professional throats were being cut left right and centre and the air was acrid with the smoke of competition. One writer, a man I hardly knew, rushed at me across the Hilton lobby on my third or fourth day in town as I was returning to my room with some FAO documentation I had managed to get hold of. He snatched the weighty reports from my hands and scanned them greedily then returned them to me with disgust as he realized they were only 'background'.

For all the journalists, the story was the thing, the story itself, intact, complete and unexpurgated. And the story was not to be found in Addis Ababa. Elusive as will-o'-the-wisp, the story was 'out there somewhere', in the field, where people were dying. It became an essential virility symbol for every correspondent to visit the field, establish eye contact with the starving, and return with the story—preferably as soon as possible. In this there were close parallels to the world of the war-correspondent. On-the-spot coverage of the famine carried much of the macho professional kudos of battlefield journalism but with none of the nasty attendant risks of being blown up by a mine, eviscerated by shrapnel, or maimed in cross-fire. You could go out there, get right in amongst the dying, see them, smell them, touch them, interview them, and then you could come back, file your story and have a first class dinner.

Neither were the journalists the only people waiting in Addis to get out into the field. Celebrities by the dozen were inundating

the hard-pressed Public Relations Office of the Relief and Re-
habilitation Commission with requests for travel permits.
Charlton Heston, Senator Edward Kennedy and Cardinal Basil
Hume were just a few of the VIPs who turned up.

Other, less important, visitors had also been enticed to Ethiopia in large numbers, the kind of people who, for want of a
precise phrase, might be termed 'disaster groupies', a new breed
of tourist for whom the conventional Third World attractions
of sun, sand, sea and sex are no longer enough. Typically these
were young, middle class Europeans, with a few Americans
thrown in. The women wore earnest expressions, but not bras,
and favoured jeans and sandals, displaying large dirty feet. The
men, fresh-faced but with aggressive beards, were equally casual
and equally earnest. What many of these people had in common
was a lack of proper visas—some had got off their Nairobi-
bound planes at Addis on impulse—and an absence of any good
reason, other than a perverse, voyeuristic urge, for wanting to
visit the famine areas. Nevertheless, they too had cast their
applications for provincial travel permits upon the still waters
of the Ethiopian bureaucracy and now waited in hope with all
the rest of us.

My own wait, thanks to good contacts and previous experience of how travel permits are granted, was not a long one.
After just a week I was making my way to Addis Ababa's Bole
Airport in the company of Tom Kelly and Dr Joseph Kennedy,
two aid workers from the American voluntary agency Africaire.
At Bole, after a brief extra delay caused by the fact that a hijacked
Somali Airlines Boeing 707 was parked on the tarmac under
imminent threat of destruction, we piled into the RRC's yellow
single-engined Cessna and took off, heading north.

Our first destination was not one of the famine areas but rather
the port of Assab on the Red Sea coast where the majority
of relief food provided by the international community enters
Ethiopia. Flying up the Rift Valley at a height of 12,000 feet,
the only visible landmark in the universe of sand and lava-flows
below was the winding course of the Awash River. Faint sugges-
tions of greenery clung to its banks, mocked by the surrounding
desert, like promises that were never meant to be fulfilled. The
further we flew, the narrower the strip of green became until,
after a few more miles, it disappeared altogether in a place where
the river poured out the last of its energy into a few stagnant,

salty pools. North from there, the terrain became increasingly burnt and withered and the gaping caldera of long-dead volcanos seemed to gaze blankly up at the sky. Close to Assab itself a parched and pitted lunar landscape of unparalleled bleakness and hostility opened up, affording glimpses of the sea like a mirage through the shimmering haze.

We landed in a fierce dust storm whipped up by the giant turboprops of one of the two RAF Hercules C130 transporter aircraft on loan to Ethiopia from Britain. Loaded with sacks of relief grain marked 'Wheat: Gift of Canada' it seemed, as it took off into the late afternoon sun, to be a potent symbol of international goodwill and organizing ability.

Assab is one of the hottest places in the world and the hardest work is done there early in the morning and just before dusk. When we arrived at the port two ships were being unloaded. One was discharging bulk commercial wheat, bought by the Ethiopian government for sale in Addis Ababa. The other was discharging bags of soy-fortified sorghum grits donated by the US charity Catholic Relief Services.

Despite the impression of activity that these two shipments gave, the alarming truth was that Assab, which is capable of handling 5,000 tonnes of cargo a day, was practically empty of food. Concerned port officials told us that unless more aid arrived quickly there would be simply nothing more to transport to the famine areas. The RAF and other planes, as well as the huge convoys of trucks marshalled by the government to move food, would all have to be stood down.

The next morning we flew to the city of Makalle, regional capital of Tigre, and a centre to which tens of thousands of famine victims have swarmed in a desperate search for food.

Our route to Makalle was a dog-leg. First northwards, following the coastline, then west across the flat and featureless desert of the Danakil depression until finally, like a monumental cliff face, the escarpment reared up sheer before us, nine thousand feet into the sky. The ground, which had been far away below, was now close, almost close enough to touch.

It would have been difficult to find a more graphic illustration of Ethiopia's varied topography. The change from lowland to highland, however, is usually accompanied by equally dramatic alterations in vegetation cover and in the colour of the land. It puzzled me to see that, here, this was not the case. The lofty

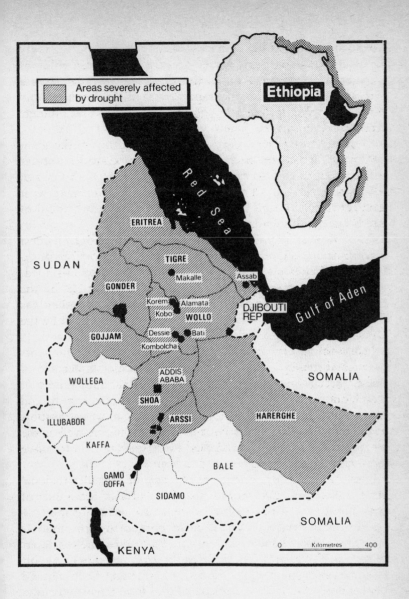

Ethiopia

Areas severely affected by drought

Red Sea

ERITREA

SUDAN

TIGRE

Makalle

Assab

GONDER

Korem
Kobo
Alamata

DJIBOUTI
REP

Gulf of Aden

WOLLO

GOJJAM

Dessie
Kombolcha

Bati

WOLLEGA

ADDIS
ABABA

SOMALIA

SHOA

ILLUBABOR

ARSSI

HARERGHE

KAFFA

GAMO
GOFFA

BALE

SIDAMO

SOMALIA

0   Kilometres   400

KENYA

terrain around Makalle, which should have been green, was the same dull, unrelieved and barren grey as that of the desert.

Where were the fields and the farmsteads, where the industrious farmers, where their wives, where their children? Looking down at the wasteland below, I knew the answer and it kept recurring in my head, a new verse to the old song: 'All gone into relief camps, every one . . . long time ago.'

Makalle airport stands on an exposed plain on the outskirts of the old city. In stark contrast to the heat and humidity of Assab, the air here, at above 2,000 metres, was cold. A morning wind was blowing, chill and bitter, and even the heavy sweater that I had brought with me failed to keep me warm.

There was a great deal of activity. A Transamerica Hercules was offloading supplies of relief grain and, as I went to photograph it, another landed in a tumult of dust and noise. Moments later a third Hercules came in—this time one of the RAF planes on its first flight of the day out of Assab. Off to one side, on an improvised apron, dozens of Soviet Mil-6 and Mil-8 helicopters were lined up being loaded with grain destined for remote parts of the province.

On the drive from the airport into Makalle we stopped to visit one of the many semi-permanent 'shelters' for drought-victims: a straggling, tented camp pitched by the side of the road. The few thousand inhabitants, predominantly women and children, gazed uninterestedly at us with the dull resigned eyes of cattle awaiting slaughter. All seemed to be covered in a layer of dust as though they had sought to bury themselves in the unfruitful earth. Like troglodytes, those who did not have tents sat in shallow scooped-out hollows in the ground. A few mothers, clutching inert rag-draped bundles, huddled behind a makeshift windbreak of dry stone where a pale fire burned.

Walking deeper and deeper into the camp I found that I had to pick my way with care through layers of humanity to avoid treading on sleeping children. As I did so, stepping slowly and deliberately forward like a sleepwalker, I found my perceptions strangely altered—as though this were, indeed, a dream. This was a state that I was to find myself slipping into again and again during the days and nights I spent in Ethiopia's despoiled northern provinces, a sense of having passed unknowingly through some door or window in the wall of reality: on one side, the world as I knew it, normal, warm, predictable; on the other side a new and terrifying universe, cold, desolate and bizarre, with landscapes and characters furnished by Hieronymus Bosch.

Now, as I walked, it seemed to me that I had fallen under the same spell, and into the same dead stupor, as those whom I had come to see. Here a mother, a toothless and wizened crone of 18 years, held to her shrivelled breast a mummified baby, more like a Chinese apothecary's specimen than a human child; here, squatting in the dust, a moulting disembodied head balanced on folded stick-like legs gazed up with sightless eyes into the pitiless sun; there, with compulsive preoccupation, a lunatic woman picked repetitively for fleas amongst the decomposing vestments of a corpse. It would have been easy, I felt, to lay myself down, listlessly scoop out my own nest of stone, and sleep for a thousand years.

As we climbed back into the RRC's Land-Rover to continue the journey into Makalle, I could see that Tom Kelly and Joe Kennedy were as shaken as I was. 'This is bad,' muttered Tom, a veteran of several famines, 'bad as I've ever seen.'

'No,' said Joe quietly, 'it's worse.'

In Makalle, we spent some time with the local representative of the Relief and Rehabilitation Commission, a man whose task of caring for the two million famine victims of Tigre seemed about as impossible as King Canute's legendary attempt to hold back the sea. He pointed out gratefully, however, that his organization was not alone: in addition to the four massive camps set up by the RRC around Makalle, the Red Cross, UNICEF, Catholic Relief Services and many other non-governmental or-ganizations and voluntary agencies had established their own feeding centres. 'Together we do our best,' he said, 'but con-ditions in the province are intolerable. There just isn't any food outside the feeding centres.'

'What sort of solution does the government have in mind for this problem?' I asked. 'You can't feed a whole province for ever.'

'The only solution is resettlement. Tigre is a very bad place for agriculture just now, but there is good land in the south of the country. Our plan is to move people from here to there.'

'How many do you intend to move?'

'At least 75,000 family heads by the end of this year, which means around 350,000 to 400,000 people if you assume that each family head has an average of four dependents. In the long-term, say by the end of 1985, we intend to move over one million.'

'What are the selection criteria for resettlement?'

'Family heads resettled have to be between 18 and 45 years old. They have to be able-bodied and physically fit. And they have to be willing to go.'

'So this is a voluntary resettlement programme? No one is forced to move?'

'Yes, it is voluntary, entirely voluntary. Our problem is not making people go, but keeping back those who have to stay. Wouldn't you also want to get away from the situation in Tigre right now? Believe me, we have no shortage of volunteers.'

Visiting the various feeding centres at Makalle it was easy to see why famine victims would seize any opportunity for a new life.

Outside a shelter set up by the Red Cross to provide supplementary feeding to severely malnourished infants some 3,000 to 4,000 mothers had gathered, each hoping that their baby would be numbered amongst the lucky hundred to be admitted that day. Nurse Greta Weichlinger told me: 'Our capacity here is for 640 children—so we have to be strict or we would just be overwhelmed. The criterion for admission is that a child should be below 70 per cent of normal body weight. Such children we then feed three times a day on a milk-based, high-protein diet of about 2,000 calories. When they are back to 80 per cent of body weight we have to discharge them so that others can be admitted.' She gestured helplessly at the expectant crowd waiting outside the gate of the shelter: 'At least it is not as hard for me as it was before to turn mothers with their babies away. A few weeks ago, before the international emergency aid really began to arrive, there was no food anywhere in Makalle and I knew that if I didn't take them in then probably they would die. Now at least, with the airlift, I believe that those I turn away may have a chance of finding food somewhere in the town.'

In the RRC's main centre at Makalle, tens of thousands of drought refugees had gathered, cramped together in a crowded, insanitary ghetto of tents and huts dumped down on a stony, litter-strewn plain. Here, as though by a bulldozer, the great human diversity that is Ethiopia had been levelled and all people were the same, destitute and crestfallen, the colour of dust, striving only to efface themselves, their very postures of defeat and humiliation seeming to proclaim: 'Do not count us; we are the wretched of the earth.'

I was shocked to find, at first indistinguishable amongst the Tigrinya-speaking highland peasants, groups of Afar nomads, men, women and children together, universally bereft of their pride, forced after facing the utmost privation to seek shelter here on the alien plateau. One Afar woman I talked to, Sittina Gharissa, told me that after the death of her husband some weeks previously she had walked a distance of almost 200 kilometres from her Rift Valley home to this place. She had brought with her her four children but one had died on the way and now another was laid low with pneumonia. 'I came because of hunger and because I heard that there was food here. My family's livestock all died—first the cattle, then the goats, last of all the camels. Finally we did not even have a cup of milk to drink. That is why I came.'

The highlanders had similar stories of destitution and lost independence to tell. One old man, Kiros Gebre-Mikael, had walked 65 kilometres to Makalle from the Shakat area of Tigre after his fields, in the third successive year without rain, failed to produce any crop. 'I planted,' he said, 'but nothing grew. I sold my ox, and continued to live for a while longer. But it was useless; there was nothing for me there. So I said goodbye to my farm and I came to Makalle.' Too old to be resettled, Kiros must stay in Tigre. I asked him what hopes he had for the future. He replied: 'I have none. Even if the rains come again my ox is gone and I have no grain to plant. Perhaps I will die here, in this camp. Who knows but God?'

In the sprawling Makalle camps, run through with epidemics of diarrhoea, pneumonia and tuberculosis, the death rate amongst the elderly is horrific. The city's small hospital has already been so deluged with the halt and the sick that it can no longer even make a pretence of practising normal medicine and has had to institute a policy of triage—concentrating its attentions on those potentially productive people whom it makes the best social and economic sense to save. In this equation the elderly do not figure at all: if they fall ill they are simply left to die.

Triage, also, is the philosophy of the resettlement programme, to which a great many famine victims are called but relatively few are chosen. On our way out of Makalle, in a reservation close to the airport, we came across a group of about 2,000 would-be migrants waiting to be driven to the runway where they would board Soviet Antonov cargo planes and be flown to new settlements in the virgin lands of Kaffa, Illubabor and Wollega. Young men and women, not yet stunned by hunger, they presented an image of hope and brave endeavour as they lined up in the sun to board the lorry convoy for the airport. It was an image that contrasted starkly with the morose fatalism of the feeding centres but that spoke equally eloquently of the end of an era and of a way of life in northern Ethiopia.

Leaving Makalle we flew due south along the edge of the high plateau towards Dessie, regional capital of Wollo, which dominates the province from a height of more than 8,000 feet. We did not land at Dessie, however, but instead veered sharply east towards the town of Kombolcha, barely 10 kilometres away as the crow flies but more than 2,000 feet lower down the side of the Rift Valley. Waiting for a squadron of helicopters to take off, we circled Kombolcha's small gravel strip, overflying, as we did so, a barren amphitheatre of land into which were set two bright fields of sorghum where the figures of labourers could be seen bringing in the harvest. 'That's a good sight,' said Tom, 'they must have had a spot of rain and timed their planting just right.'

Two fields, however, cannot feed a province, and the rest of Wollo was as bare as bone.

From Kombolcha, we drove east to Bati along 40 kilometres of winding road that took us yet another 1,000 feet down into the Rift. This was a sentimental journey for me because I had travelled the same route only 18 months before, a time when famine in Wollo seemed at worst a remote and far-off threat.

Then all the fields had been ripe with grain and the road had been thronged—in places blocked—with Afar cattle and camels on their way to the Monday market at Bati. Now the picture was very different. There were no cattle at all, other than a few picked-clean carcases glaring whitely at the sun, and of all those great camel herds I remembered I now saw only three mangy beasts, their ribs protruding through poor coats, searching amongst the acacia thorns for sustenance. Worst of all was the denuded wilderness of the fields. As far as the eye could see in all directions nothing was growing. Surrounding the derelict farmsteads, the thin, shorn stubble of blighted and blackened sorghum, which even the wheeling crows had left, seemed the product of some cataclysmic scorched-earth policy, the final solution of a land's despair.

'It's desert,' I heard myself say. 'Nothing will ever grow here again.'

Tom Kelly and Joseph Kennedy disagreed and I could guess that they had perhaps found the site for the Africaire project they were planning for Ethiopia. 'It looks like a desert,' Tom said, 'but the desertification isn't too far advanced. It's on the cusp. The topsoil could still be saved. In this kind of situation the right kinds of small-scale, long-term development programmes could still work wonders. With proper soil-conservation and water-shed management techniques this land could become productive again.'

Despite Tom's optimistic, and almost certainly accurate, assessment, I was feeling profoundly depressed by the time we arrived in Bati. Of course, I was prepared for the fact that the market would be long gone—trade is the passion of happy and prosperous people and goes out of fashion when human life itself has lost its value. Nevertheless, the change that had overtaken this once bright and animated town was very difficult for me to come to terms with. It was as though a veil had been drawn down over the sun or as though, in a reversal of the Biblical process, I now saw 'through a glass darkly' a Bati that had become a dim and deformed reflection of its former self.

A huge expanse of open land to the south west of the town had been taken over as a billet for the drought refugees. So rapid had their influx been, however, and on such a large scale, that there had been no time to build proper pit latrines or take even the most rudimentary sanitary precautions. The air, pungent with the reek of human ordure, was alive with dense swarms of flies. A generalized malaise seemed to hang over the camp, a fetid, almost tangible miasma of death and disease.

Inevitably, in such conditions, it was the children who suffered the most: marasmus and xerophthalmia were commonplace, killing the weak, blinding and maiming the strong, blighting a whole generation. Dysentery, tuberculosis and pneumonia, those other hand-maidens of the apocalypse, had also taken a fearful toll. The few doctors at the camp were labouring frantically in a last-ditch effort to check the spread of epidemics that might slaughter thousands, or tens of thousands, in a night.

The Red Cross supplementary feeding centre—nothing more than a long, tin-roofed shack—was like an image of the most infamous of the Victorian workhouses. Into this pestilential den, a thousand mothers with their sickly infants had crowded and now sat torpidly in the warm shadowy light awaiting the gift of food. The air was filled with a low murmur of sound, at first not unlike the hushed whisper of a congregation before the minister arrives but soon recognizable as being composed of the feeble cries of dying babies and of a pitiful, continuous, consumptive coughing.

Exhausted nurses and paramedical staff, walking wearily through this densely-packed mass of troubled people and doling out rations to those children still able to take food by mouth, were clearly at the limits of their endurance, at a loss to cope with the scale and complexity of the human damage they faced. Walking with them, I felt numb, stunned, dizzy. Hot, bony fingers grasped at me in puny supplication as I passed and it was only with the utmost difficulty that I prevented myself from running away. Hours later, to my shame, I found myself washing my arm where it had been touched—as if, in that citadel of the damned, I had been infected with some dangerous and creeping contagion.

The 30,000 drought refugees at Bati now far outnumber the original inhabitants of the town. Gathered from a wide catchment area, they come predominantly from poor farming families, people whose lives are eked out on the extreme margins of subsistence, a grim economic borderland where the slightest climatic upset can mean utter destitution.

Outside the supplementary feeding centre I talked to one such victim, Idris Yousuf Ali, who left his farm and made his way to Bati in October 1984: 'My life was always hard, always difficult,' he told me, 'but somehow I survived. Ten years ago, in the last great drought, I had to sell almost all my possessions; but at least I managed to remain on my farm. This time the drought was worse, and I could not stay.' Asked if he thought he might be able to go back to farming at some time in the future, his words echoed those of Kiros Gebre-Mikael at Makalle: 'How can I go back when I have nothing to go back to? Once I had a good store of seed grain. I planted it in expectation of the rain—but there was no rain, the crop did not grow, and the seeds rotted in the ground. Once I had four oxen for ploughing and of these, when there was no food left to eat, I sold two and slaughtered two for meat. So you see, I cannot go back. I have eaten my future.'

The shared predicament of Idris Yousuf Ali and Kiros Gebre-Mikael reflects a widespread, and so far unannounced, disaster in Ethiopia that is going to continue long after the present drought is over. In many areas the whole agricultural sector, to which nine-tenths of the Ethiopian population belongs, has simply *stopped*. For it to start again, hundreds of thousands of individual farmers are going to require not only the onset of the rains but also the essential inputs—draught oxen, seed grain and simple tools—that make farming possible. More than this, both those who are resettled in the south and those who remain in the north are going to require a great deal of well-organized technical assistance to enable them to make the best of their respective environments. Beyond emergency feeding, therefore, the damage wrought by the drought means that there is now an urgent need for sustained, long-term development aid to the agricultural sector in Ethiopia, the kind of aid which, so far, the international community has been most unwilling to give.

Food aid alone is just not enough. It does not return peasants to their farms. It does not provide the hungry with the means to feed themselves. This is not to say, however, that food aid is unnecessary—because the contrary is true. I finished my visit to the famine areas of Ethiopia quite certain that, had it not been for the shipments of emergency food that began to arrive in October 1984, many hundreds of thousands of people who are still alive today would certainly have died.

The difference between life and death, health and sickness, is no more than a thin thread. And while it is true that international emergency assistance prevented many from crossing that border-line from the light into the darkness, it is equally true that there were many for whom the help came too late.

This was the case in the remote mountain lands in the north-western corner of Wollo province, between the historic city of Lalibela and the small town of Korem, where the devastation of the drought was at its most extreme. Politically unstable as a result of frequent TPLF incursions, difficult of access by road and by air, conditions here quickly deteriorated in the second half of 1984 as the crops failed for the fourth successive season. The meagre public stores of grain, already heavily depleted in previous years, were quickly exhausted and people throughout the region began quietly, uncomplainingly, and with great dignity, to starve. As a result, when the first truckloads of food aid arrived in Korem in November, the death toll had already run into tens of thousands.

When I visited Korem, at the beginning of December 1984, the situation had stabilized somewhat but people were still dying in droves. The only difference, according to aid workers, was that they were now dying in relief camps rather than on their farms and that there was therefore some hope that the death-rate might be brought under control.

Flying to Korem from Kombolcha it was easy to observe the scale of the ecological problem that the region faced, and to understand why so many people had starved here. Along the entire route there was not a single patch of green to be seen: not a single grassy meadow, nor a single field of *teff*, relieved the cheerless monotony of the landscape. The nearer we drew to Korem the more dreary and desolate the dun-coloured vistas became and the abandoned farms and the empty villages that we saw seemed to us like the leavings of a long-dead civilization, a mystery that archaeologists of the future might ponder over and ask, 'what strange calamity happened here?'

Korem has no airstrip of its own so, to get there, it is necessary to land at the town of Alamata in the valley a few thousand feet below and then drive 25 kilometres of winding road up a mountainside.

The valley in which Alamata stands was, within living memory, a fertile and well-watered *shangri'la* where a variety of crops grew in abundance. Today it is a barren, depopulated wasteland, the colour of old cement, where a few skeletal trees by the side of dried-out river beds are the only reminders of past wealth. Across it all a dry wind blows. Summoned by this wind, dust devils spiral heavenwards and vacuum up the last of the topsoil. Transported to the ionosphere this topsoil, in which the hopes of a proud people were once planted, darkens the days, turns the yellow sun crimson and obliterates the stars.

While we waited by the Alamata airstrip for transport to take us to Korem, Tom Kelly said: 'You come into this and you think, "God, what a beautiful agricultural valley this should be." The land looks like at one point it was so good that people probably took it for granted. I guess they farmed it without much care for how they were treating it. They ploughed it up willy-nilly and allowed erosion to take place. They planted the wrong kind of crops that deprived the soil of nutrients. Then the droughts came and the people got desperate and they ploughed up the land some more, more than it could take. That was what happened in the States, in Oklahoma, in the 1930s and I guess that's what has happened here. Maybe what we're seeing in Ethiopia is the Dustbowl all over again. . . .'

The comparison is an apt one, except that Ethiopia's Okies have no obvious California to flee to. Perhaps in the new settlements of the south they will be enabled to start again; but, in the meantime, countless thousands remain trapped in the godforsaken north in camps and feeding centres that collectively constitute an Abaddon on earth.

Alamata itself was crammed with drought refugees. Some were so weak that they had simply lain down where they stood, blocking the main road. Others, not yet so far gone, restlessly roamed the back streets like wolves in search of food, eyes staring from their heads, their lips drawn back in grimaces of ferocious hunger.

On the drive out of Alamata the air became progressively colder so that, although shirt-sleeves were all that were needed on the valley floor, sweaters and anoraks had to be pulled from our luggage before we reached the mountain top. Then, as we arrived in Korem, it began to rain—a cold drenching drizzle too late by far to be of any use to the dispossessed farmers of Wollo but representing a new and terrible threat to the 60,000 drought victims camped in the exposed fields outside the town.

Looking back on Korem now, my mind shies away from the terrible things I saw there and I find it difficult to write. It was, for me, a vision of the end of the world. I remember thinking that when our politicians finally lose their heads, when the ICBMs are released from their silos, and when the nuclear winter descends, then this is what we, the privileged citizens of the industrialized nations, will at last discover that we have brought down on ourselves. The lights will go out across Europe and, in a hundred thousand Korems, a new dark age will be born.

It is nigh on impossible to describe the total and abject despair of those benighted people, strewn like the casualties of some brutish medieval battle across the blasted heath that constitutes Korem main camp. The children were in a worse condition even than those at Bati, while the adults, with huge bald heads atop dwarfish, skeletal bodies, seemed to be not of this earth and resembled more a science-fiction artist's grotesque conception of a colony of Martians than anything remotely human.

In the dust behind a relief food truck that passed through the camp, I witnessed a child grubbing for a few grains of corn that had fallen to the ground. And I saw a group of men, drooling and licking their lips in hungry anticipation, smash up and gnaw the horns and skull of a cow.

But at least there was food in Korem—even if pitifully little of it—and people no longer faced the immediate threat of death by starvation. Far more serious, at an altitude where temperatures below freezing point are common, was the fact that 30,000 people, about half the population of the camp, had *no shelter whatsoever,* no blankets, no waterproof clothing and, in the total absence for miles around of any fuelwood, no fires. Huddled together for warmth, indistinguishable in their common misery, men, women and children, the old and the young, journeyed into each night like the victims of some terrible sacrificial rite. Even as sleep came, each was possessed by the certain knowledge that, come morning, many of their number would be dead—that, in the cold hours before dawn, loved ones would pass away, and, worse even than this, that there was nothing, absolutely nothing at all, to be done. The remorseless mechanism of these deaths from exposure, the cruel process whereby each new day would bring its fresh crop of 100, 200, perhaps 300 corpses, sickened me to the heart. It was all so avoidable, so unnecessary —a few lorryloads of tents and blankets would have made the difference.

The camp is a wintry hell, but it is less of a hell than the countryside that surrounds it.

Thus it was, as Christmas came and went, and as 1984 edged into 1985, that upwards of 500 drought refugees *every day* were continuing to pour into Korem, compounding and complicating an already stupefying logistical problem for the overburdened relief agencies. Many other camps, including those at Bati and Makalle, also continued to grow in size rather than to diminish, despite the outflow to the new settlements and to the graveyards. Indeed, by January of the New Year, it was obvious that Ethiopia's famine, far from showing signs of improvement, was in fact getting steadily worse.

Like a cancer, it had spread outwards from Tigre and Wollo to take possession also of most of the provinces of Gonder and Eritrea, and parts of Gojjam, Shoa and Arssi. There were also reports from the United Nations High Commissioner for Refugees that the drought had extended into the giant lowland eastern province of Harerghe threatening the lives and livelihoods of more than one million nomads. Successful development programmes started since the end of the Ogaden war were, according to UNHCR Ethiopia representative Colin Mitchell 'now at risk of being totally destroyed. . . .' Families, he said, were roaming the countryside with their animals in search of food and pasture, and cattle were dying from exhaustion and dehydration after being driven for hundreds of miles. If drastic measures were not implemented immediately, Mitchell warned, there would be 'a disaster in Harerghe on no less a scale than in Wollo and Tigre.'

All in all, by January 1985, the Ethiopian famine was estimated to be affecting upwards of seven and a half million people and, at a time when the 'emotional shelf-life' of the disaster had probably already come to an end as far as the interest and attention of the Western public was concerned, the need was for ever greater assistance and generosity. As Relief and Rehabilitation Commissioner Dawit Wolde-Ghiorgis told a meeting of donors:

The arrival of grain, supplementary food and other relief items must be vastly increased, and the words of the hundreds of visitors the RRC has hosted over the last two months must be translated into the arrival of grain at the ports, the filling of regional and sub-regional stores with the grain, and the immediate distribution of this grain into the hands of those who need it now and who will need it over the coming months. It is only if this happens on a much-increased scale that the present tragedy will be overcome; if it does not happen, the situation will deteriorate to a horrifying and almost unimaginable extent, and the world will have on its conscience the responsibility for a catastrophe which it could so easily have prevented.

PART THREE

What Can Be Done; What Should Be Done

CHAPTER SEVEN

The International Reaction:
Bigger than Kampuchea

In Britain and other Western European countries, in the United States and Canada, and in Australia and New Zealand, public response to the Ethiopian famine in terms of charitable donations was quite unprecedented. As Oxfam's Marcus Thompson commented: 'It's the biggest ever for us. It has overtaken Kampuchea.'

In Britain alone, by mid-November 1984—less than a month after news of the famine had first broken—Oxfam was able to report that its Ethiopia appeal had already raised over £2 million. Thanks to the early warnings of its field officers, Oxfam had despatched 14,000 tonnes of wheat to Ethiopia in September and, with the new money available, it was now possible to follow this up with further shipments and with deliveries of special 'high-energy biscuits'—65 tonnes of which reached the starving of Korem in the first week of November. Oxfam also sent out two expert nutrition teams, each three persons strong, to work in the famine areas.

In the same short period, Save the Children Fund's appeal also raised £2 million. Initial action included the despatch of seven British staff to join a team of 60 Ethiopian nutritionists working at Korem. A shipment of 1,500 tonnes of milled wheat was purchased (and subsequently delivered in Assab in early December). Twenty-one tonnes of high-energy foodstuffs were also immediately flown to Addis Ababa.

Christian Aid had raised £1 million by mid-November of which £650,000 was immediately distributed—mostly in the form of cash grants to relief organizations working in guerrilla-held areas of Eritrea and Tigre. Likewise War on Want allocated most of the £620,000 that it raised in this period to Eritrea and Tigre: 1,000 tonnes of grain arrived at Port Sudan during

November for delivery by lorry to the guerrilla-held areas and a further shipment of 4,000 tonnes was on the way.

World Vision of Britain raised £160,000 within three weeks of the October television news stories and sent most of this to its Addis Ababa office to supply and service five feeding and medical centres in Wollo, Shoa and Gonder. In the same period the British Red Cross raised £500,000 of which £230,000 was immediately spent on an airlift of urgently needed stoves, tents, bedding and feeding equipment for Bati camp.

To the surprise of many aid workers, the initial charitable response of the public did not melt away during November and December. On the contrary, it snowballed—which perhaps had something to do with the fact that the traditional 'season of good will' had arrived. The hit record 'Do they know it's Christmas' was just one of a number of ingenious measures that raised millions of extra pounds in a matter of weeks and, by January 1985, the total 'take' of the British charities from their Ethiopia appeals stood at a staggering £25 million.

Indeed, so great had the attraction of Ethiopia been to donors that other charitable causes were suffering. Britain's National Society for the Prevention of Cruelty to Children, for example, experienced a shortfall of 30 per cent in funds received during this period, and Sir John Cox, director of the Spastics Society, reported that his team was having to work much harder to bring in its £11 million yearly income because of the Ethiopia fund-raising campaign.

In general, however, the feeling amongst the voluntary agencies was that the Ethiopia appeal had played an important role in raising public consciousness to the predicament of the less advantaged and that as such—whatever the immediate effects on charities whose work was unrelated to Ethiopia—the long-term impact would be positive. Fergus Logan of Mencap summed up this view when he said that he thought the 'fairly spectacular public support' for the Ethiopia appeal might have encouraged people to donate money who did not usually contribute to the charity 'pool' at all.

Public sympathy for Ethiopia found particularly spectacular expression in the activities of a number of British newspapers which made major efforts to help the hungry and to boost circulation at the same time. The *Sun*'s campaign 'Give a Tiddler to save a Toddler' produced £100,000 for Save the Children

Fund in its first week of operation. 'The *Sun* and its readers will be saving the lives of hundreds of children who would otherwise have died,' commented Hugh MacKay, the charity's Director, on 29 October 1984. Upstaging the *Sun*'s effort, the *Daily Mirror* airlifted almost £1 million worth of food to Ethiopia at the beginning of November, amidst soaring headlines which proclaimed: 'THANK GOD YOU'VE ARRIVED'. Correspondent Alastair Campbell wrote:

> I was with the *Mirror*'s mercy mission when it reached journey's end as our convoy rolled into the tragic town of Korem, home for 60,000 starving men, women and children. Within minutes of the first ten-ton Volvo lorry pulling up in the heart of the country's biggest feeding station, it was besieged by hundreds of emaciated, yet beaming children. Charity workers, who have been fighting a losing battle against death and disease, were overjoyed. A Save the Children Fund spokesman said: 'Thank God you've arrived'.

The fund-raising successes of the charities and the press were not the only indicators of the strength of public sympathy for the victims of the Ethiopian famine. There were also many stirring individual sacrifices made, and actions taken, which would have been notable under any circumstances but which were all the more remarkable for having been inspired by a tragedy in a far-off Third World country. One couple in Scotland sold their mobile home and almost all their personal possessions in order to send money to Ethiopia; a Cambridgeshire farmer, Oliver Walston, persuaded many other farmers to donate a tonne of wheat each—and raised 1,000 tonnes in November 1984 alone; a Barnstaple man, Leslie Garland, raised over £10,000 for Oxfam by collecting from passers-by in a shopping centre near his home, until the local council stopped him for being in technical breach of a bylaw; postmen in London and the Home Counties made free deliveries during December 1984 of six million Save the Children Fund envelopes for the Ethiopia appeal.

The compassionate response of the British public to the Ethiopian famine, the widespread desire to *help* the victims, was typical of what was happening around the world. In late October 1984, for example, immediately after the BBC film revealing the true extent of the famine had been networked in the United

States, sympathetic Americans began to inundate relief agencies with offers to help. 'The telephones have been ringing constantly,' said Mr James Sheffield, president of the United States Committee for UNICEF. 'Many are in tears when they call. They've seen television footage. They call and say it's horrible and something must be done.' Contributions were averaging $40 per person and the United States Committee said that it had never before seen such an outpouring. 'A lot of people who call don't even know where Ethiopia is,' said Mr Sheffield. 'They don't know how to spell it. But they're horrified by the tragedy.'

In Europe, public outrage at what was going on soon developed beyond mere horror at the tragic scenes picked up by the television cameras and took on a political complexion. In a way that had never happened before with any other Third World disaster, people began to question the policies of their own governments towards Ethiopia and to demand action from reluctant and laggardly bureaucracies. As Marcus Thompson observed:

> The new element, as I see it, is that whereas in the past we have had people responding to a tragic situation with sympathy and generosity, there is, in this case, also an element of anger. It coincides with bumper harvests here. It coincides with a government in Ethiopia that gets very little response from Western governments normally. And as I see it, the really new element in the Ethiopia story is that there is an overwhelming demand that governments address this problem with the surpluses that they have available here. There is a recognition that voluntary agencies, such as Oxfam and Save the Children Fund, Christian Aid, CAFOD and others can do what they can do; but when it comes to a million tonnes of grain needed over a year then that is out of our league. Accordingly, there is a recognition that there is a need for political action by John Citizen in the street with his MP to get governments and the United Nations to intervene. If we can put a man on the moon, and all these things, then surely we can get rid of bumper harvests in Europe and America to people who are starving in Ethiopia?

Indeed, 1984 *was* a bumper year for agriculture: at the height of the Ethiopian famine, the International Wheat Council called a press conference in London to announce a record harvest of 509 million tonnes, and the UN estimated world cereal production at 1.761 *billion* tonnes, up eight per cent on 1983. At the same time, it was revealed that the EEC was sitting on a stockpile of 8.7 million tonnes of cereals on which storage charges alone were running at £25 per tonne per year.

Commenting on the paradox whereby Europe could hoard surpluses while millions of Ethiopians starved, Timothy Phipps, Deputy Director General of Save the Children Fund, said: 'There is an embarrassing, disgusting mountain of grain, wheat and millet all over Europe, which ought to be released in massive shipments.'

On 30 October 1984 the London *Daily Mail* published a photograph of the contents of one of the EEC grain warehouses and observed:

> This picture is a staggering example of how thousands of tons of grain are being stockpiled, because of EEC regulations, while millions starve. It was taken at a warehouse near Swindon, Wiltshire, where 100,000 tonnes of surplus wheat and barley—enough to feed the starving of Ethiopia for six weeks —is heaped high. The glut this year is so great in Britain alone that the hunt is on for extra warehouses to take in the load.

Public anger at the miserliness of Western governments was eloquently summed up in a letter to the London *Daily Express* from one reader, Mrs M. Devine of Eastcote: "Most Western Heads of State, including the American President, keep telling us they are God-fearing Christians—so why don't they act with greater generosity in sending more from their surplus food mountains to Ethiopia?"

Overnight, food aid had become a voting issue. As a result, governments that had hitherto shown nothing but indifference to Ethiopia's plight suddenly began to take an interest. Immediately after television coverage of the disaster began, Britain's Overseas Development Minister promised £5 million for emergency programmes, 6,000 tonnes of food, and two Hercules aircraft to help with deliveries. A few days later, on 31 October 1984, the EEC announced a package of £34 million worth of emergency aid for Africa—most of it for Ethiopia. And on 16 November the United States said that it had decided to send $37.5 million worth of food to Ethiopia.

Neither was this kind of reaction to public pressure confined to governments of the West. The Eastern Bloc, which has given almost no development aid to Ethiopia at all over the last decade, also jumped heavily onto the humanitarian bandwagon. After an initial media blackout on the subject, reports of the Ethiopian drought began to appear in the Soviet press early in November and soon a big emergency shipment of rice was announced, along with trucks and vehicles worth £850,000. Russia also seconded a large number of heavy-transport aircraft. On 12 November it was reported that Bulgaria had sent two aircraft loaded with food and medicine to Ethiopia, and would follow up with a ship carrying heavy equipment including tractors and trucks. At the same time, East Germany pledged 3,000 tonnes of food, as well as medicines and blankets, and began immediate deliveries by air.

Soviet Bloc food-aid during the emergency fell, as always, very far below that provided by the West, and looked paltry and mean beside the huge US grain shipments that got under way in late 1984. Nevertheless, though different in degree, capitalist and communist styles of assistance had one important characteristic in common: both were 'crisis reactions' to a much-publicized disaster, and both were largely confined to providing short-term aid to famine victims. There was no serious attempt, on either side of the Iron Curtain, to give Ethiopia the kind of help—for example in soil conservation and agricultural development programmes aimed at helping farmers to boost productivity—that would enable it to avoid future famines.

By the beginning of 1985, at least in the West where people are free to criticize the policies of their governments, this was the issue to which concerned development agencies were addressing themselves. Nobody was disputing the value of food aid in itself, or the absolute necessity for it in Ethiopia; but the argument was being forcefully advanced that emergency assistance was not enough and that Ethiopia should be allowed to benefit from long-term help after the emergency was over. Only if that happened could the basic development problems that had caused the emergency in the first place begin to be resolved.

As Lloyd Timberlake of the environmental pressure group Earthscan commented:

It is all very well to dump food, blankets and tents on people after a disaster. But what you have really got to do is get the money spent *before* the disaster. People who respond with a sort of convulsive emotion to dying children have got to be brought to realize that their money can be better spent improving the lot of those children *before* they get into such an awful state—before they become terribly malnourished and on the brink of death.

Elaborating on this theme, an Oxfam leaflet entitled 'Ethiopia is Hungry for Change' observed:

Ethiopia has areas of good quality land. Experts reckon that food production could be tripled with the right sort of soil and water conservation, and Oxfam-supported projects have demonstrated that such increases of yields are possible EVEN IN THESE DROUGHT YEARS. It's impossible to make rain fall to order, but it is possible to make drought more tolerable and manageable. Severe soil erosion, deforestation and declining yields continue in the most-affected areas because few resources have been given to long-term development. Ethiopia desperately needs aid from the rich world, to increase food production and to prevent famines in the future. But little of this aid is forthcoming. BRITAIN SHOULD LIFT ITS BAN ON LONG-TERM DEVELOPMENT AID TO ETHIOPIA.

An identical point was made by Christian Aid and by the Catholic Fund for Overseas Development in a joint presentation to Britain's House of Commons Foreign Affairs Committee. Speaking of famine in Africa in general, the agencies said that they were critical of the failure of governments and of the international system to respond to the crisis with long-term as well as emergency aid: 'The most significant example is Ethiopia, where the UK government's rush to make emergency resources available took place in the absence of any bilateral development programme in that country.'

In their effort to win long-term aid for Ethopia, the British voluntary agencies quickly received the support of a number of Members of Parliament. Said Tony Baldry, Conservative MP for Banbury: 'We want to see a sustained, co-ordinated, long-term campaign of help. There have been 10 years of failure by both West and East to prevent the current disaster.'

However, support was lacking where it was needed most. Both Britain's Prime Minister, Margaret Thatcher, and the Overseas Development Minister, Timothy Raison, declared themselves steadfastly against committing any long-term aid at all to Ethiopia.

Like Britain, the United States gives emergency 'humanitarian' assistance; but it is not involved in any bilateral development projects in Ethiopia and has repeatedly stated that it will not countenance long-term aid to a country that it sees as the Soviet Union's key satellite in Africa. Indeed, Washington's loathing for Ethiopia's Marxist government is so extreme that even its humanitarian aid has to be delivered circuitously, through the medium of the voluntary agencies: no American food is handed over directly to the Relief and Rehabilitation Commission.

The result of this attitude has been that, in the one area of potential 'humanitarian' assistance which might have had positive long-term implications for Ethiopian development—the resettlement programme for victims of the drought—both Britain and the United States have refused to become involved.

At a donors' meeting in Addis Ababa on 11 December 1984 the RRC requested international help for its resettlement efforts, including transport to move would-be migrants from the north to the south of the country. This request was ignored by Britain and unequivocally turned down by America. 'We do not want to have any part of it,' said one US aide. The next day, at a news conference in Washington, Peter McPherson, Chief Administrator of the US Agency for International Development, explained why. Ethiopia, he said, should stop its resettlement programme immediately because 'the money and resources should be used to help the millions facing starvation'.

Was this wilful stupidity? Did Mr McPherson really believe that a perennial food dole was the only answer to Ethiopian hunger? And could he really not see that resettlement, probably more than any other single strategy, holds forth the hope of rehabilitating large numbers of destitute Ethiopians and giving them the chance to become productive once again?

CHAPTER EIGHT

The Ethiopian Reaction: Millions on the Move

Significantly, while the United States 'does not want any part of it', resettlement is one of the few aspects of long-term development in Ethiopia that the Soviet Union has shown itself willing to become involved with. One may speculate that this is because the concept of treating human beings *en masse* as material resources to be transported here and there according to the dictates of central government planners appeals in some special way to the Russian mind. Whether or not this is the explanation, however, there is no doubt that the fact that Soviet planes with Soviet pilots have participated heavily in the human airlift out of Tigre and Wollo has only served to distance the West further from what is, essentially, a sound and worthwhile development strategy. More than this, it has encouraged a number of observers to see in the resettlement programme elements of a sinister conspiracy. As War on Want Director George Galloway wrote in the *Spectator* on 1 December 1984: 'Most ominously, the *Dergue* are now proposing to "resettle" some two and a half million people from the "infertile", i.e. rebellious, north to the "fertile", i.e. less troubled, southern regions—and they are asking the West to pay for it.'

Mr Galloway need not have worried. His articles and several others like them, as well as the protests of the Tigre People's Liberation Front, have found support in the policies of the British and American Governments, neither of which is going to 'pay' one penny towards the cost of resettlement. As the *Guardian* of 20 December 1984 observed, US officials are convinced that the programme is nothing more than an attempt 'to disperse the guerrillas and the population which supports them.'

When I arrived in Ethiopia in November 1984 to begin my own visits to the famine-affected areas, the resettlement airlift was already well underway—and I was deeply suspicious of it.

It seemed to me, I suppose, rather too convenient and neat that the very provinces in which the security problem posed by the TPLF was most serious—Tigre and Wollo—should also be the provinces scheduled to provide the largest supplies of human fodder for the resettlement programme. First starved half to death, then divided up in scattered communities all over southern Ethiopia, the contumacious northerners would no longer be in any position to oppose the government.

As I began to travel in Tigre and Wollo, however, to visit the feeding centres and, most of all, to see for myself the total devastation of these two provinces, my suspicions subsided. After the flight to Korem, and after witnessing the horrific scale of human misery there, I became convinced that resettlement was necessary. All my subsequent researches have confirmed this view and I have come to regard the refusal of Britain and America to assist the programme as a spiteful and misdirected error.

To be sure, one motive behind resettlement might indeed be to deprive the TPLF of grass-roots support—but whether or not this is the case is a matter of purely academic conjecture. The more important fact is that vast areas of the north have become uninhabitable wastelands on the verge of total, irreversible ecological collapse. In the words of Robert Lamb of the United Nations Environment Programme, Wollo and Tigre 'have been so overfarmed, overgrazed and deforested that efforts to scrape a bare living from this land threaten to destroy it completely.' Given this state of affairs, the hard reality is that resettlement of a large segment of the population is imperative. The only alternative is mass starvation—this year, next year, and in every year to come—and hopeless, everlasting dependency on international food hand-outs. In short, without resettlement, the 1984 emergency will become a permanent condition. As Lloyd Timberlake of Earthscan commented when interviewed during the preparation of this book: 'I think people have got to be resettled. I think it makes sense to try to get people out of an area which simply can't support them and where there is no way it can support them, into an area which can support them— and one hopes that it can be done efficiently, intelligently and humanely.'

Inevitably, there have been accusations that the Ethiopian government is forcing northerners to move to the new settle-

ments against their will. These accusations have stemmed, notably, from Peter McPherson of US AID, from War on Want,
and from the TPLF which, in late November 1984, began to
hijack lorries being used to carry migrants. I can only report my
own findings from random discussions with the destitute at
Korem, Bati and Makalle, and from talks with Ethiopian friends
whose opinions I trust, that these accusations are incorrect. Far
from being forced, my impression is that the majority of the
drought-affected people strongly *want* to go. And this impression, I know, is shared by many voluntary agency personnel
who have spent months working with the famine victims. As
Oxfam's Marcus Thompson commented: 'It is certainly not
wholesale forced resettlement. Our teams who have been in
Wollo have seen and met people who are eager volunteer re-
settlers waiting to go elsewhere.'

The immediate aim of the resettlement programme is to move
300,000 families (about 1.5 million people according to official
Government figures) from what Ethiopia's Relief and Rehabilitation Commissioner describes as 'the over-populated and overused highlands of the north to the unused or underused land in
the south and west.' According to Mr Wolde-Ghiorgis, the
programme

is actually a shift of the relief centres from scorched and arid
environments to environments conducive to relief programmes and to the eventual complete rehabilitation of the
victims. . . . The movement of people from one relief centre
to another is entirely voluntary, and rehabilitation programmes will start with the allocation of individual holdings
of land within existing peasants' associations. By taking these
measures, the government is giving support to and organizing
the spontaneous internal migration which is now being observed in many parts of the country. Recently, some 2,900
people crossed Addis on foot from Wollo region on their way
to western Ethiopia. This spontaneous reaction of people
manifested in the form of disorganized movement, unless
properly managed and organized, will result in an undesirable
situation. . . . Therefore by organizing and expediting the
movement of people from drought-stricken areas to areas that
are less prone to drought, the government is taking up and
sharing the responsibility for actions which the people have

taken by themselves. In time, and with the proper agricultural inputs, these families should not only be self-sufficient in food but also producing a surplus.

Resettlement is not a new concept in Ethiopia. The first efforts in this direction were made in the early 1960s and a total of 20,000 families were enrolled in various government-supported schemes by 1974. After the revolution, however, the programme was speeded up. An official Settlement Authority was established in 1976 and its functions were later merged with those of the Relief and Rehabilitation Commission in 1979. By the beginning of 1984, prior to the new and massive influx occasioned by the drought, a total of 83 settlements, all relatively small-scale and with a combined population of approximately 160,000, were in operation throughout the country.

Assosa, situated in grassy, low-lying land on the western edge of the province of Wollega some 700 kilometres from Addis Ababa, is typical of many of the new settlements. Established in 1979 with 6,000 settlers, its population had grown to 21,458 by early 1984. During these first five years a total of 5,135 hectares of land were cleared, ploughed and planted with a diversified range of food and cash crops including 2,143 hectares of maize; 1,021 hectares of sorghum; 705 hectares of haricot beans; 347 hectares of *teff* (Ethiopia's indigenous grain); four hectares of mixed sunflower/rape; and 287 hectares of pepper and spices. In addition a long-term afforestation project was started with more than one million tree seedlings planted on an area of 472 hectares. Though predominantly agricultural, the settlement possessed some 3,000 goats and sheep, and 4,000 chickens at the beginning of 1984 and, with financial support from Oxfam, had begun to purchase and vaccinate modest numbers of cattle.

In late 1984, as Ethiopia's resettlement programme began to speed up in response to the drought, Assosa suddenly found itself hosting very large numbers of new migrants. Aid workers and agricultural experts warned that the arrival of thousands of destitute people from Wollo and Tigre could be disruptive if not properly handled; however, they also agreed that, with the right kind of inputs and development assistance, there was no reason why Assosa should not be able to support an expanded population of 50,000 or even more.

The scale of the resettlement programme is so big that the kind of aid Ethiopia requires for it cannot possibly come from the voluntary agencies;* direct government-to-government help is what is needed. At the beginning of 1985, however, it was precisely this sort of help which Britain and America, with their enormous resources, were leading the way in denying to Assosa and to all the other settlements like it. First the RRC's December 1984 request for assistance in transporting migrants was turned down. Then, shortly afterwards, its appeal for essential inputs —agricultural machinery and land-clearing equipment, oxen, seeds, and pesticides—was also rejected out of hand.

Clearly in its settlement activities, as in all other aspects of long-term development, Ethiopia is going to have to get by without the major bilateral assistance that Western governments normally extend to projects in developing countries. Despite all the public sympathy generated in Britain, America and elsewhere as a result of the emergency, official policies towards Ethiopia are going to stay as unhelpful and as uncompromising as ever. The country might get some extra food but its position at the bottom of the Third World league as the lowest per capita recipient of development aid is not going to change.

The resettlement programme, although it is an important part of Ethiopia's response to the challenge of hunger, is only one aspect of a wide-ranging strategy. This strategy, whether it relates to moving people out of drought-affected areas, or helping those who stay behind to lead more productive lives, has consistently failed to attract the kind of support that it needs from the international community.

In Wollo for example, at the height of the famine, two RRC schemes aimed at increasing crop yields and improving land use had to be cut back as a result of shortage of funds. The first of these, the Kobo-Alamata Agricultural Development Project, had been making considerable progress in encouraging farmers to plant drought-resistant varieties of sorghum and other crops. The second, at nearby Sirinka, had been attempting to rehabilitate eroded escarpments through integrated land use involving water-resource management and reafforestation. The projects had been started with money from the Federal Republic of

---

*The recent airlift of Falashas (Ethiopian Jews) to Israel is estimated to have cost $300 million.

Germany—one of the Western governments that has excepted itself from the general rule of not giving long-term aid to Ethiopia—and from the World Bank, a multilateral agency. In late 1984, however, after appeals for further funding had failed, Sirinka was closed down entirely. Likewise, since the £300,000 needed to keep Kobo–Alamata going for another year was not forthcoming from any source, activity on this project had to be drastically curtailed and it seemed unlikely that it would survive long into the New Year.

The RRC's efforts aimed at managing the fragile ecology of northern Ethiopia, and at reversing the harmful effects of centuries of misuse, have received widespread support from environmental experts. As Lloyd Timberlake of Earthscan commented:

> The government has organized the peasants into peasant associations which now include, I believe, seven million people. Through the medium of these associations, they are doing precisely the right sort of thing. They are trying to alter these lands so that they retain soil, retain water, and can better stand up under drought conditions. . . . You just can't do what you need to to the countryside to save it from disaster until you organize the peasants, as in China and South Korea and parts of India. Ethiopia is about the only African country doing this.

Ethiopia's land reform programme, of which the setting up of peasant associations was an integral part, was less than a decade old when the 1984 drought hit the country. In this time, however, the associations had planted 620 million trees, built over 110,000 kilometres of terraces on eroded northern hillsides, and, in Wollo alone, had completed 20 irrigation projects with an average size of 600 hectares.

While these kinds of successes in environmental action demonstrate what a mobilized peasantry can achieve, it must also be reiterated that the management of the agricultural sector in Ethiopia still leaves much to be desired.

Though organization of the peasants and the massive redistribution of land that took place after 1975 have both been very positive factors, Ethiopian agriculture today suffers from the blind application of ideology by dogmatic bureaucrats who often know absolutely nothing about farming or the mentality and needs of rural populations. The country's state farms, for example, which have absorbed huge amounts of investment, are for the most part inefficient and unproductive white elephants that would be best closed down. As one agricultural expert, John Empson, writing in the *Financial Times* of 12 September 1984, observed of Ethiopia's state farms: 'They lose money, even when given higher prices than those paid to peasants. They also use up too much of the scarce resources of capital and skill.' In this respect at least, Peter McPherson of US AID is right when he says that the Ethiopians should 'rethink their collectivized-farming approach—an export from the Soviet Union which doesn't work back at home and doesn't work in Ethiopia.'

Another profound problem, shared with many Third World nations, is the over-emphasis that the government of Ethiopia puts on the growing of cash crops for export. The larger co-operatives and state farms devote their best land to coffee, the principal foreign exchange earner, while food crops are relegated to less productive areas.

At the same time, in order to keep food prices low in the cities (where the cost of bread is a sensitive political issue) small farmers are paid unrealistically low prices for their crops of sorghum and *teff*. This discourages them from making the kind of investments that might boost production and Ethiopia becomes increasingly less able to feed itself. The deleterious effects of this policy of paying low producer prices, described in one FAO document as exchanging 'later shortages for present short-run advantage' cannot be overstated.

As a result of these problems, compounded by war and drought, the agricultural sector as a whole in Ethiopia has grown at only 2.5 per cent a year since the revolution (slower than the rate of population growth), and, although some cash crops have done well, food production has actually regressed. There are now signs, however, that Ethiopia's leaders, notably Head of State Mengistu Haile Mariam, are coming to regard this situation as unacceptable and that policy changes to promote increased output may be on the way. As one FAO report notes, development of the agricultural sector has recently been 'assigned the highest priority'.

It is to be hoped that political considerations will not forever

deter Western governments from extending long-term assistance
to agriculture in Ethiopia, since it will be largely through the
judicious development of this sector that the challenge of hunger
will be met. The creation of many separate small-scale projects
that make maximum use of the human resources already available within the peasant associations may be the strategy that
will hold forth the best hopes of success, particularly if the
government can be persuaded to pay higher prices to producers
in order to encourage greater output. In the absence of such
development, famines will continue to threaten the lives of
millions of Ethiopians from year to year and dependence on
international food aid will become a permanent feature of the
country's economy and way of life.

In the last quarter of 1984 avalanches of food began to pour
into Ethiopia as European and North American surpluses were
released. Perhaps inevitably at such a time, it was not long before
accusations began to be heard that the government was misusing
this aid, selling it, giving it to troops and in various other ways
preventing it from reaching the famine victims for whom it was
intended.

Once again, George Galloway of War on Want was among
the first to start raising the alarm:

> By now it is clearly incontestable [he wrote in the *Sunday
> Times* of 2 December 1984] that huge amounts of aid delivered
> to the Ethiopians are somehow ending up on the black market.
> As ITN films showed last week, a train of camels laden with
> grain, skimmed milk and other foodstuffs is trekking each
> night from behind Ethiopian lines, stopping at selected mer-
> chants, and heading ultimately for an illegal border crossing
> into Sudan.

In a similar article in the *Spectator* the day before, Galloway
informed his readers that

> a huge misappropriation of Western food aid is currently
> taking place. In one village, Girmaica, I personally photo-
> graphed sacks of powdered milk, the free gift of the people of
> Canada, West Germany and the United States. . . . I watched
> it being loaded on the backs of a long camel train and setting
> off at night to cross the border illegally into the Sudan. Later

I saw it for sale in the Sudanese town of Kassala. The case that Colonel Mengistu is using British taxpayers' money . . . to oil the wheels of his bankrupt economy by selling food aid is overwhelming.

In fact the case is not overwhelming at all. No doubt there is a black market in food aid in Ethiopia; with such large quantities arriving it would be surprising if there were not. Mr Galloway has every right to draw attention to the extent of this black market that he witnessed. What is regrettable, however, since he did not suggest in his articles that there was any counter-evidence to his accusations, is that many of his readers may have generalized from the particular instances he cited and assumed, with him, that a 'huge misappropriation' of Western food aid was under way. Such assumptions, in turn, may have discouraged potential donors to the Ethiopian appeal. As Marcus Thompson of Oxfam pointed out when asked about such reports:

> Certainly a lot of people will have seized on this and more or less said to themselves 'oh well, they're all crooks so I needn't put my hand in my pocket to help'—and this is a very unfortunate side effect. We say in this field that whenever there is a lot of mud being slung around some of it always sticks. Then the relief operation suffers.

Oxfam discounts almost entirely the accusations and insinuations about misappropriated food aid in Ethiopia: 'We sent a senior overseas accountant from here to audit the distribution system and procedures of the Relief and Rehabilitation Commission and he found them conscientiously implemented and was very satisfied.'

If the RRC's distribution work is so good, however, then how do stories like Galloway's get started? Surely they have to be based on something?

According to Thompson, the accusations concerning mis-appropriated food have three main points of origin and these have to be taken very carefully into account:

> First of all, you have to remember that there is political conflict in Ethiopia so, obviously, each side has a propaganda operation against the other, and obviously each side will be putting out

propaganda stories about how bad the others are and how they abuse things and misuse things . . .

The second point to keep in mind is that a lot of Western food aid is delivered in very good-quality bags which have stamped on the side 'Gift of the People of the United States, Not to be Sold', or whatever. Now these bags when they are empty of their first cargo are sold in the market or are bought up—I don't know which—by the quartermaster of the military supplies or whatever. He uses the empty bags to put whatever he wants to put into them, and then a journalist or somebody sees these bags going somewhere clearly that the first cargo that the bag contained was never intended to go to. Then we get a whole lot of stories started up which are quite wrong. The bags are simply being recycled and it's unfortunate that you can't overprint what's written on them.

The third point is that if you distribute stuff to people, you must allow the recipients the right to cash in what they are given if they have other priorities. If you give a bag of grain to somebody and he wants to buy medicine for his wife or he wants to buy school books for his children or clothes for his family, and he trades some of the grain which he has been given because it's perhaps surplus to his immediate need or he feels he has another priority, you can't then criticize the aid agency that gave it by saying 'We saw some of your stuff on sale in the market', because the recipient has legitimately decided that he wants to sell some of it. . . . In any relief situation, there will always be a market in the commodity which is being given away.

Once these three factors are taken into account, the alarming stories about food aid going astray in Ethiopia start to look less damaging. As Tony Baldry, Conservative MP for Banbury, observed in a letter to the *Sunday Times* in the week after Galloway's report:

This is not the first time that such allegations have been made, and on each and every occasion when they have been investigated the allegations have been found to be without substance. In July 1981, and again in June 1983, European Parliament delegations visited Ethiopia and reported that the country was making responsible and effective use of the food and other aid provided by the European Community and that there was no evidence to suggest that aid was going astray. This was also confirmed by a later report of the Commission of the European Community.

On this point, Marcus Thompson, a man with considerable experience of the relief operation in Ethiopia, wholeheartedly agrees:

> Oxfam has no brief for the Ethiopian government and we don't want to whitewash the situation. All we can say is that our observations from our experience in the country have been good. We have found the Relief and Rehabilitation Commission to have made the most strenuous efforts to deliver relief aid to people in the famine-affected areas. . . .

CHAPTER NINE

In Search of a Solution: Hungry for Change

The challenge of hunger in Ethiopia encompasses the world. Across the emaciated bellies of the dying children of Korem are tattooed the military strategies and the trade and aid policies of the big powers. To attempt to succour those children without also seeking to restructure the global order is to do little more than treat the symptoms of the disease while ignoring its fundamental causes.

This is not to argue that feeding is unnecessary. On the contrary, in the present situation in Ethiopia, food aid is a vital, humanitarian must. It is, however, a call for recognition of the fact that the problems of hunger run long and broad and deep, that they extend beyond simple drought and crop failures, and that the industrialized nations are heavily implicated.

There is a growing recognition that change is necessary. This awareness has, in part, been sparked off by the Ethiopian famine which seems to have politicized the thinking of many who were shamed and distressed by the cruel paradox of record grain surpluses in Europe at a time of mass starvation in Africa. This led to forceful demands being made upon politicians that the surpluses should be released; it also helped to forge new attitudes towards aid policies in general.

In Britain, aid spending as a percentage of gross national product is already lower than that of almost every other European country. The UN target of 0.7 per cent has never been reached and, in the last ten years, successive governments have determinedly whittled down what the British give so that it now stands at just 0.35 per cent of GNP. At the height of the Ethiopian famine, sure that the British public would remain as apathetic as ever, Overseas Development Minister Mr Timothy Raison was poised to institute yet another major cut in the aid budget. He was surprised—and obliged to backtrack considerably—

by the furore that this plan caused. As the London *Observer* commented at the time:

> The aid cuts now being contemplated by the government demonstrate how far out of touch it can be with public sentiment. It takes a special degree of ineptitude, or insensitivity, to consider taking millions of pounds off the government's aid budget at the very time when the public, stirred by the harrowing pictures of starving children, is flooding relief agencies with notes and cheques to save lives in Ethiopia.

Neither was the new level of public awareness confined to the demand that the quantity of aid given should not be reduced. There was also an understanding that the *quality* of assistance mattered, that gifts of food were not enough and that the total absence of any British development aid programme in Ethiopia was a scandal. A Neilsen opinion poll commissioned by Oxfam in November 1984 showed that 74 per cent of the British people thought that the main purpose of government aid should be longer term development to prevent famine. As Oxfam's National Campaign Manager John Clark commented: 'The poll reflects the overwhelming support of the British people for aid to the poor and demonstrates the depth of public understanding of aid priorities.'

Public understanding of aid priorities, however, while it is to be welcomed, is only one of many steps that will have to be taken if the challenge of hunger in Ethiopia is ever to be met. As this book has attempted to show, attitude and policy changes are also required in several other areas.

First and foremost, the horrific arms race in the Horn of Africa must somehow be brought to an end. A main battle tank costs $2.5 million and a multi-role combat aircraft costs $30 million. These are toys that Ethiopia, in its present state of underdevelopment, simply cannot afford. The hard fact is, however, since it is in the nature of governments to rule, that Ethiopia's leaders are going to go on investing in such weapons of destruction as long as they face insurrection in Eritrea and Tigre. Covert Western support for the EPLF and the TPLF—largely via the Sudan—has prolonged these conflicts and has contributed to the destabilization of a whole region. This support is hypocritical in the extreme. No Western government is prepared to tolerate domestic insurrection—witness the presence of British troops in Northern Ireland—or to support guerrilla movements that threaten pro-Western Third World regimes—witness El Salvador. Western encouragement for the EPLF and the TPLF should therefore cease and maximum pressure should be applied to bring these groups to the negotiating table as quickly as possible.

Secondly, Ethiopia suffers persistent underdevelopment because, in common with many other developing countries, the terms of world trade are weighted heavily against it. As Hans Dell, FAO Resident Representative in Ethiopia, points out:

> It is a fact that some countries, or groups of countries, will have a food deficit. Others will produce more than they need. This is where trade comes in. . . . As an example, my country, Denmark, has no natural mineral or energy resources, but it has the conditions for good agricultural production. So it produces the dairy products which buy the steel and energy which are needed to build the ships, which are sold to buy the oil, etc, etc. Likewise, a country like the Soviet Union is not producing sufficient food to feed its population. But there is no food shortage, because the Soviet Union produces oil and other commodities which it sells, so it can buy the millions of tonnes of grain every year which it needs to feed its population.
>
>   It is a fact, however, that this system has broken down when it comes to the so-called developing nations. For a number of reasons, the world economic situation has, for the time being, put an end to the 'trade-on-equal-terms' system. The world market is in fact flooded by the traditional export commodities of the developing countries. Coffee, sugar, rice, cocoa, tea, natural fibres, tropical fruits, wood, cotton, nuts, and many other commodities—which often are produced as the only crop or product from a given country—are fetching less and less in comparison to the price of oil and processed industrial goods. In general, the prices of goods from developing countries have fallen about 20 per cent since 1960, whilst the prices of necessary imports have risen sometimes 100 per cent or more. As an example—in 1974, 10 units of coffee would buy one unit of oil, today 100 units of coffee are needed to buy the same measure of oil.

In such a situation, caused by forces that are totally outside its own control, it is inevitable that Ethiopia must get poorer and poorer. Further, as it devotes more and more of its good land to coffee and other cash crops in order to pay for its imports, it is equally inevitable that it will become less and less able to feed itself. The figures bear this out. The export value of Ethiopian cotton tripled between 1976 and 1981. Similarly, between 1975 and 1983, coffee production increased by 20 per cent and sugar-cane production by 36 per cent. These advances, were, however, achieved at the cost of food production which grew at less than two per cent a year, and were virtually negated by the increased costs of imports—in other words, despite exporting more and more, Ethiopia has not even managed to maintain its trading position of 10 years ago.

One way to help solve this problem is to campaign for better terms of trade for developing countries like Ethiopia, to insist that our governments take part in international commodity agreements which offer fair prices for Third World commodities and to insist that these prices be stable and predictable. As Oxfam's Nigel Twose points out:

> Price fluctuations make economic planning a nightmare for the exporting countries. With so many countries being encouraged to produce the same export crops (those which are wanted in the rich countries), it is easy to set them in competition against each other. The result is that companies in rich countries can stop buying from one country temporarily, to force prices down. One classic example occurred in 1975: the United States bought 100 million dollars worth of sugar from Brazil but the following year bought none and, instead, increased sugar purchases from the Philippines three times over. In the same two year period, exactly the same thing happened with cotton: the United States purchased 50 per cent less Mexican cotton and 90 per cent less Pakistani cotton than it had the previous year, but bought four times as much Indian cotton. Such practices may keep prices low for the purchaser, but five-year plans become meaningless if a government does not know what its budget is likely to be from one year to the next.

A third factor in the poverty that renders Ethiopia so unable to deal with the problems of drought and famine is debt. As well as being heavily in hock to the Soviet Union—something about which we in the West can do nothing—the country also owes our own banks one billion US dollars. Interest payments on a sum of this size, borrowed at commercial rates, are, needless to say, astronomical and currently cost Ethiopia in the region of 20 per cent of all its export earnings.

Ethiopia's debt problem, like almost all its other development problems, is something that it shares with much of the rest of the Third World. And Third World debt as a whole is now so large that defaulters could in theory bring down the international financial system. Western banks have therefore done everything in their power to avert the threat of big debtor nations like Mexico or Brazil declaring themselves unable to repay; these manoeuvres, however, have actually worsened the position of really poor countries like Ethiopia, and particularly of the very poor within those countries.

International finance is currently policed by the International Monetary Fund which, throughout the Third World, seeks to oblige governments to implement 'adjustment programmes' aimed at reducing expenditure while at the same time building up the productive base of the economy. Although this sounds sensible enough, IMF-style policies tend to have catastrophic consequences for those at the bottom of the pile in countries where the starting point is very low. As Nigel Twose observes:

> Adjustment programmes generally include, in part, import reductions which lead to reduced economic activity and higher unemployment. They also include credit ceilings being imposed on both the public and the private sectors; in the short term at least, this increases unemployment and reduces real wages. Government expenditure is reduced and the targets of such cuts are invariably the social services and food subsidies. . . . But it is not just the austerity measures which affect the poor. As far as food needs are concerned, the major result of an IMF intervention in the Third World is the acceleration of changes in agricultural practices, resulting in even greater concentration on crops for export, at the expense of food crops for local consumption.

Anyone seeking to help solve the challenge of hunger in Ethiopia should campaign for a reduction in interest rates and for an overall reduction of the country's debt burden. At the same time, those international institutions which *do* provide cheap finance to the developing countries—for example the International Development Association—should be supported. The IDA, which is the soft-loan affiliate of the World Bank, gives interest-free loans, or very low-interest loans, repayable over 50-year periods, to the poorest countries. Early in 1984, however, the United States dramatically reduced its own contribution to the IDA and used its political muscle to persuade other donors further to starve the Association of funds.

As Oxfam observes:

> The poor are being brought into a world food system in which the crude power of economic forces prevails over all moral considerations . . . It appears that the governments of the rich countries are unwilling to negotiate meaningfully on the key issues which would allow governments of the poor to work towards food self-sufficiency for all. Without change in the world trade system, producers will never get a fair return for their commodities. Without change in the terms of loan repayments, the poor's food supply will remain in jeopardy. Without change in aid programmes, smaller farmers' attempts to grow their own food will become increasingly unsuccessful. And without change in the agricultural policies of the rich world, poor countries will continue to be encouraged to produce more and more export crops to help us to create market gluts.

It is comforting to be able to feel that we have done our duty towards the starving of Ethiopia by giving a few pounds or dollars to one or other of the emergency appeals. We have not, however, and unless we are also prepared to campaign for change in all the major structural problems that underlie world hunger, we should not pretend to ourselves that our donations are worth very much.

Yet how can we, as individuals, possibly hope to change the world? Is it just wishful thinking to suggest that we can do anything at all?

Oxfam, at least, does not believe that such thinking is wishful and has recently launched a campaign 'Hungry for Change', which it hopes will expand public awareness of the complex causes of underdevelopment, and, through expanding awareness, promote political action. This campaign is not solely about Ethiopia but, rather, makes the point that Ethiopia's problems are best understood in the wider context of Third World poverty and of an unjust global economic system. In the absence of other such initiatives, probably the best single step that any individual wishing to help Ethiopia could take would be to join 'Hungry for Change'.

Oxfam's logic in launching the campaign is worth quoting at length:

We have all seen the horrifying pictures of Ethiopia today. But severe hunger is not confined to that one corner of Africa; 500 million people go hungry every day (that's the size of the entire population of Europe). Yet, in the rich world, many are reluctant to acknowledge responsibility; instead they prefer to blame world hunger on a convenient set of myths:

'*There's not enough food.*' Wrong. The world produces enough food to give every person on earth a nourishing 3,000 calories a day.

'*There are too many people.*' Wrong. Holland has 1,079 people per square mile, while Brazil, where thousands go hungry, has 39.

'*We've got food mountains, why can't we send more food?*' We shouldn't. Food aid is essential for emergency relief, as in Ethiopia, but as a development tool it can upset local market prices and slow down the progression towards people feeding themselves. In reality, hunger is a condition which is fuelled by the influences and forces of rich countries like our own:

AVARICE: In 1973 the price of oil doubled twice. Commercial banks, overwhelmed with surplus funds, channelled massive loans to the Third World and saddled them with floating interest rates. These interest rates have since soared so high that they have crippled many of the poorer nations. To cope with this crisis, these nations have been forced to make heavy cuts. And in human terms, the sacrifices have been severe. Health and social services, already basic, are now seriously threatened. Food prices have risen dramatically. Wages have been reduced. And work is disappearing. These austerity measures have had a dire and often fatal effect on the poor.

   GREED: The developed nations, comprising 30 per cent of the worlds' population, consume over 80 per cent of its resources. (Not because they need to; the UK alone swallows over £500,000,000 worth of slimming aids every year). To satisfy this greed, and at the same time pay the interest rates, developing nations have been forced to grow more crops for export. Consequently, land that should be feeding their people is producing food for European and North American consumers. And thousands of acres are devoted to growing crops for European livestock, whose milk and butter end up as part of the rich world's food mountains. These systems lead to deprivation for millions. Scarcely able to feed themselves, the poor face a daily struggle to survive. Many don't. Every single day, 40,000 children die as a result of hunger.

   APATHY: Little can change while so many in the developed world remain indifferent. In 1983, the share of UK income devoted to aid dropped to almost the lowest level for 20 years. How many even knew? It is apathy which allows these injustices to persist. . . .

Perhaps the Ethiopian famine has taught us that we can be apathetic no longer, that we cannot simply stand by and watch fellow human beings destroyed by avoidable hunger. Korem, Bati, Makalle—all have reminded us of a lasting truth: that we live in an interdependent world and that, in such a world, it is unacceptable for millions to starve while others prosper.

No man is an Island, entire of itself; every man is a piece of the Continent, a part of the main. . . . Any man's death diminishes me, because I am involved in Mankind; And therefore never send to know for whom the bell tolls; it tolls for thee.

                                     (John Donne, 1571-1631)

Select Bibliography

A large number of publications were consulted during the preparation of this book. The following are particularly recommended for further reading:

The Ethiopian Revolution, Fred Halliday & Maxine Molyneux, Verso Editions, London 1981 & 1983.

Ethiopia's Revolution, Raul Valdes Vivo, International Publishers, New York, 1978.

Conflict and Intervention in the Horn of Africa, Berket Habte Selassie, Monthly Review Press, New York and London, 1980.

Conflict in the Horn of Africa, Colin Legum & Bill Lee, Rex Collings, London 1977.

Natural Disasters: Acts of God or Acts of Man? Anders Wijkman & Lloyd Timberlake, Earthscan, London, 1984.

Various publications of the Relief and Rehabilitation Commission, Addis Ababa, Ethiopia, including, specifically:

Review of the Current Drought Situation in Ethiopia, December 1984; *Drought Situation in Ethiopia, and Assistance Requirements 1984/ 85,* October, 1984;

Review of Current Situation in Drought-Affected Regions of Ethiopia (April–July), August 1984;

Early Warning System Report 1984 Meher (Main) Season Production Prospect, September 1984;

Introductory Statement at Donors' Conference, by Chief Commissioner Dawit Wolde-Ghiorgis, October 1984;

Introductory Statement at Donors' Conference, by Chief Commissioner Dawit Wolde-Ghiorgis, December, 1984.

The Great Ethiopian Famine of 1888–1892. A New Assessment, Richard Pankhurst, *Journal of the History of Medicine,* 1966, Volume XXI, No. 2.

The History of Famine and Pestilence in Ethiopia prior to the Founding of Gonder, Richard Pankhurst, *Journal of Ethiopian Studies,* Addis Ababa, 1972, Volume X, No. 2.

Eritrea and Tigray, Minority Rights Group Report, London 1983.

Cultivating Hunger: An Oxfam Study of Food, Power and Poverty, Nigel Twose, Oxfam, Oxford, 1984.

Lessons to be Learned: Drought and Famine in Ethiopia, Oxfam, Oxford, 1984.